Developing
Media Literacy
in Cyberspace

# DEVELOPING MEDIA LITERACY IN CYBERSPACE

Pedagogy and Critical Learning
for the Twenty-First-Century Classroom

## JULIE D. FRECHETTE

Westport, Connecticut
London

**Library of Congress Cataloging-in-Publication Data**

Frechette, Julie D., 1971–
    Developing media literacy in cyberspace : pedagogy and critical learning for the
twenty-first-century classroom / Julie D. Frechette.
        p.   cm.
    Includes bibliographical references (p.    ) and index.
    ISBN 0–275–97578–9 (alk. paper)
    1. Computers and literacy.  2. Media literacy.  3. Mass media in education.  4.
Internet in education.  5. Critical pedagogy.  I. Title.
LC149.5.F74   2002
371.33'4—dc21      2001058099

British Library Cataloguing in Publication Data is available.

Library of Congress Catalog Card Number: 2001058099
ISBN: 0–275–97578–9

First published in 2002

Praeger Publishers, 88 Post Road West, Westport, CT 06881
An imprint of Greenwood Publishing Group, Inc.
www.praeger.com

Printed in the United States of America

∞™

The paper used in this book complies with the
Permanent Paper Standard issued by the National
Information Standards Organization (Z39.48–1984).

10 9 8 7 6 5 4 3 2

For Hayden and Connor

I also want to express my gratitude to
Dr. Joshua Meyrowitz
for his continued guidance, support, and inspiration.

# Contents

Tables     ix

Preface     xi

Acknowledgments     xiii

Introduction     xv

1   Reconceptualizing Learning for the Cyber-Classroom     1

2   The Political Economy of Cyber-Media     13

3   Moving Beyond Literacy Theory     23

4   Easy Solutions for Complex Problems: Internet
Restrictions and Resources     43

5   The Limits and Benefits of Technology Initiatives in
Massachusetts Schools     57

6   Empowerment over Censorship: Using Media Literacy in
Cyberspace     75

Conclusion     117

Appendix A    1998–1999 Massachusetts Lighthouse
Technology Grants: Project Summaries     123

Appendix B   Bloom's Cognitive Domain of the Taxonomy of
             Educational Objectives                        133

References                                                 135

Index                                                      143

# Tables

| | | |
|---|---|---|
| 5.1. | Lighthouse Technology Grants | 59 |
| 5.2. | Lighthouse Technology Grants: Language Arts | 59 |
| 5.3. | Lighthouse Technology Grants: Technology | 60 |
| 5.4. | Lighthouse Technology Grants: Science | 61 |
| 5.5. | Lighthouse Technology Grants: Social Studies | 62 |
| 5.6. | Lighthouse Technology Grants: Math | 62 |
| 5.7. | Lighthouse Technology Grants: Business | 63 |
| 5.8. | Lighthouse Technology Grants: Art/Graphic Design and Music | 63 |
| 5.9. | Lighthouse Technology Grants: Interdisciplinary Programs | 64 |
| 5.10. | Lighthouse Technology Grants: Foreign Language/ESL | 64 |
| 5.11. | Lighthouse Technology Grants: Special Education | 65 |
| 5.12. | Lighthouse Technology Grants: Assessment | 65 |
| 6.1. | Five Basic Questions and Concepts of Media Literacy | 99 |

# Preface

While thumbing through an educational magazine, I came across an advertisement for a technology company that read, "Never before has so much technology and information been available to mankind [*sic*]. Never before has mankind been so utterly confused." I think it would be fair to say that such an assessment sufficiently describes the current fixation with computer-mediated communications technology. Although Internet technology is no longer a novelty, educators are still scratching their heads, wondering exactly how to embark upon this new cyber-frontier for learning. *Developing Media Literacy in Cyberspace* is based on my belief that, in the age of electronic information overload, the Internet-supported classroom must incorporate media literacy in order to help students become critical citizens. Unlike measures to block or filter online information, students need an empowerment approach that will enable them to analyze, evaluate, and judge the information they receive. Although most online "safety measures" neglect to confront the emerging invasion of advertising and marketing directed to children and youth, media literacy in cyberspace demands such scrutiny. Accordingly, this book will allow us to explore the means through which technological access is deployed in order to discover what it means to be literate in the information age, as well as how to initiate cyber-literacy while transforming the learning process.

# Acknowledgments

The perspectives and research reflected in this book are the product of dialogue with friends, colleagues, mothers, students, teachers, mentors, and advisers. I'd like to begin by acknowledging that this book represents a revised version of my doctoral dissertation at the University of Massachusetts, Amherst. Thus my primary debt of thanks goes to the teachers, mentors, and advisers who supported my research at the university. I first wish to express my deepest gratitude to Leda Cooks, whose scholarship and personal words of encouragement enabled me to learn a lot about the complexities, dynamics, and politics of education. I attribute much of my success and confidence as a scholar to her guidance. I'd also like to thank Justin Lewis, whose critical perspectives, detailed feedback, and continued support also carried me through my studies. Special thanks to Lenore Carlisle, whose insights as an educator, principal, professor, and mother were integral to the success of my research.

There are many other teachers, scholars, mentors, and advisers who deserve to be mentioned, including Lisa Henderson, Jane Blankenship, Barbara Cruikshank, Michael Morgan, Sut Jhally, Carolyn Anderson, and many others. I'd also like to thank Norman Cowie for enabling me to develop my approach to media literacy through production and outreach, as well as Susan Douglas and Len Masterman, with whom I had the great fortune of coming into contact through the Five College Summer Institute in Media Literacy. Most importantly, I owe a sincere thanks to Joshua Meyrowitz, whose constant mentoring, friendship, and scholarship have inspired me since the days of my undergraduate studies.

For the personal support of my colleagues and friends, I'd like to thank Melissa Click, Nina Huntemann, and Katie Lebesco. A heartfelt thanks to Paula Gardner, Kristen Tillona, Sharon Davenport, Lisa Krisoff-Boehm, Kristen Waters, and Helena Semerjian, who clearly understand the delicate balance between mothering and scholarship and have encouraged me to succeed at both.

Thanks to my coworkers in the Department of Communications at Worcester State College—Carlos Fontes, Don Bullens, Alta Carroll, Bill Byers, Linda Fuller, and Norma Butrym—for their faith in my scholarship, teaching energies, and ability to complete my book.

Most of all, I am truly grateful for the love and support of my husband, Darryll, who has encouraged me throughout the research and writing phases of my work. I dedicate this book to my most enthusiastic supporters: Hayden, who was born during the first year of my master's program, and Connor, who patiently waited to enter our lives until I finished my Ph.D. comprehensive exams. Their sweet voices and laughter, explorative nature, and tenderness have taught me that the best pedagogy comes from love, nurturing, trust, and companionship.

# Introduction

Technology and education are two issues critical to the future of our country. Technology will continue to play a bigger role in the education of our children, whether through electronic libraries or computers—in the classroom or at home.
—Chairman William F. Goodling, Committee on Education and the Workforce

As we enter the twenty-first century, few would question the growing importance of telecommunications technology in the classroom. During his administration, President Clinton pushed to have all schools in the United States connected to the Internet by the new millennium, propelling most schools to acquire the necessary technology for Internet access. According to figures presented in a joint hearing before the Committee on Commerce and the Committee on Education and the Workforce in the House of Representatives, funding for telecommunications services has increased more than 2,000 percent since 1995 (Committee on Commerce & Committee on Education and the Workforce, 1998). At the time of the hearing, almost 80 percent of America's schools were said to have been wired to the Internet, a significant increase from 35 percent four years prior. Even without subsidies designed to provide schools with a reduced e-rate for the Internet, access to the Internet quadrupled between 1994 and 1996.

According to Market Data Retrieval, Inc., the latest figures indicate that roughly one out of five schools in the United States has a home page on the World Wide Web, and a new Web site is created about every four seconds (Sistek-Chandler, 1999, p. 15). As Cynthia Sistek-Chandler explains in "To HTML or Not to HTML?" (1999), some experts project there will be over one billion Web sites in the next few years. She states, "Web page design is now so easy even an 8-year-old can construct one" (p. 15).

As exciting as these buoyant and bright-eyed prospects of technological development and production within schools may be, many educators, administrators, government leaders, parents, and citizens remain skeptical of the significance of these technological strides. Unlike Clinton's optimism, a more cautious tone has emerged from President George W. Bush with regard to Internet restrictions in public schools and libraries. Across the country, parents and schools have approached cyber-travel with concerns about racist Web sites, pornography, pedophiles, and the like. From schools, to the government, to the computer industry, there has been a concerted effort to "cyber-patrol" the Internet. According to *Education Week*, schools and libraries that receive federal money for Internet connections had a deadline of April 16, 2001, to draft Internet safety policies, which include usage agreements, audit-tracking devices, and software filtration devices such as Surfwatch and Netnanny (Trotter, 2001). Do such solutions adequately prepare today's youth for safe cyber-surfing?

Only temporarily. In fact, it could be argued that the cyber-safety crisis dominating public policy and mainstream media coverage has produced a cultural climate ripe for the commercial exploitation of vulnerable parents and educators. While sales for software filtration programs have skyrocketed, educational ventures in cyberspace have been halted mid-flight. As Chairman Tom Bliley retorts, telecommunications services in schools are "good, but we need to know that all these programs are put to proper and effective use" (Committee on Commerce & Committee on Education and the Workforce, 1998, p. 2). Likewise, Chairman William F. Goodling believes we must "look to ensure that educational technology resources are managed and coordinated in ways that maximize learning and teaching" (p. 3).

Given these concerns, many educators see the need for integrating critical literacy skills, or information literacy, into the curriculum so students are properly trained for global electronic travel. Today's youth must learn not only how to acquire the information they desire, but more importantly, how to make sense of it. As newspaper columnist Brian Loverenz puts it, the focus should *not* be to wire schools for instant access to this electronic marvel; rather, students must first pass their driving tests—on the Internet (cited in Bundy, 1997).

One means of teaching students "driver education" on the information superhighway is to employ a media literacy curriculum framework. Popularly defined as "the ability to access, analyze, evaluate, and produce communication in a variety of forms," media literacy is the exploration and critical examination of the deluge of mediated messages we receive daily in visual and/or textual form (Leveranz & Tyner, 1993, p. 21). Media literacy offers us a way to become "literate" in visual and popular texts, giving us the tools through which to examine the political, cultural, historical, economic, and social ramifications of the media (Frechette, 1997, p. 2). As Deborah Leveranz and Kathleen Tyner (1993) explain, media literacy, or media education, begins "when the reader mentally questions mediated information in books, on television, and in all sorts of pop culture messages" (p. 21). As educational institutions have recognized rather than challenged cultural shifts from print to visual communication, media literacy has been steadily growing in the United States. However, even the most progressive educational initiatives have not gone far enough in critically analyzing nontraditional media. The time has come to provide the means for media literacy in cyberspace.

Not only is a media literacy approach to telecommunications technology vital to the integrity of critical student learning, but the traditional role of the teacher as the "fountain of knowledge" must be reconsidered as massive amounts of information are readily accessible on the Internet. As Dr. Alan Bundy articulates to teachers and librarians in his keynote address on information literacy (1997), the rate of growth of knowledge is such that the curriculum will always be behind. With the continued emergence of new technologies, learning will be less about knowledge residing in the head and more about learning the pathways to knowledge. Thus, nondidactic teaching methods are essential as libraries equipped with the Internet have improved access to data and information resources.

Accordingly, in order for students to become lifelong learners, nontraditional classroom strategies or pedagogies need to be devised and utilized in order to transform conceptualizations of education from teaching to learning through cyberspace. These questions and observations deserve considerable attention and need further development so that students can become "critically autonomous" in the next millennium.

This book will allow us to address questions centered around the integration of new telecommunications technology in the classroom by responding to concerns over Internet access and content through media literacy initiatives. While much research about online computer technology focuses on the communication *end goal* of accessing the information superhighway, we will explore the *means* through which technological access is deployed, essentially asking the questions:

What does it means to be literate in the information age, how can information literacy be initiated, and how can the learning process be transformed?[1]

This book is divided into six chapters. Chapter 1 begins by outlining the strengths and limits of computer technology within pre- and post-secondary education. It includes recent communication and educational scholarship about telecommunications technology, as well as theoretical visions about online technology and classroom learning. Next is an examination of how the nature of pedagogy changes with the introduction of decentralized technology, namely the Internet, since traditional power-structured classrooms that use a "banking system" of education are eroding under the increasingly powerful current of information consumption on the Internet.[2] As James Schwoch, Miriam White, and Susan S. Reilly (1992) articulate, exploring the pedagogy of media culture is so vital to building a "critical citizenship" because contemporary media culture is a major site of everyday learning. Although it is certainly true that the proliferation of photographic and electronically produced images and sounds serve as a form of perpetual pedagogy, we will interrogate the notion of "critical citizenship" by asking: (1) Who has access to Internet technology? (2) How has the Internet been utilized or conceptualized within the classroom curriculum? (3) What do we mean by "critical citizenship" as articulated within the theoretical frameworks of critical pedagogy and media literacy? and (4) What epistemological assumptions, forms of authority, or modes of signification are produced and/or altered through this medium?

In order to address such questions, Chapter 2 begins to investigate the administrative, educational, and parental concerns that exist regarding the use of telecommunications technology in the classroom. Such an analysis will allow us to contextualize the polemic surrounding Internet technology in the classroom so that we may better understand how issues of privacy, exploitation, and inappropriate content on the Internet are articulated within mainstream media, educational technology magazines, and cyber-communities.

Chapter 3 situates and clarifies the key terms and theoretical perspectives articulated within the body of this book. While most discussions of education and cyber-learning examined within the purview of the previous chapters establish research initiatives and modes of thinking through *literacy* theory, the underlying theorizing applicable to the present research needs to go further by correlating broad matrices of discourse in media literacy, critical pedagogy, and critical cultural studies. By identifying the theoretical gaps existent within the current conceptions of literacy and education, we will be able to establish an analytic definition of media literacy in relation to current debates about the nature and purpose of learning about, and through, multi-communication forms. This will help us articulate and advance the position in the next chapters that media literacy must include the utilization and analysis of new telecommunications technology in the classroom.

In Chapter 4, a framework of political economy is developed in order to address how current discussions of and quasi-solutions to "cyber-paranoia" uphold or benefit a commercial (technological) system designed to sell a product. By engaging in a comprehensive analysis of Internet restrictions and resource rating systems, restrictive software products, usage agreements, and adult monitoring, we will assess the benefits and limits of these initiatives. Furthermore, we will discover how the emergence of a hegemonic discourse surrounding concerns about Internet use in the classroom—including privacy, exploitation, and inappropriate content—is constructed and/or maintained within U.S. mainstream press and cyberspace communities to uphold a market-driven policy of commercialism.

Chapter 5 provides the content analysis and assessment of various technological initiatives devised, implemented, and funded in Massachusetts schools. Although Internet use is not examined through direct observations or experiments, it remains important to explore existing programs designed by educators and classroom teachers to incorporate computer-mediated innovations into the existing curriculum. This section analyzes seventy-four federally funded Lighthouse Technology Grants administered in the 1998–1999 academic school year through the Massachusetts Department of Education. The survey includes: (a) the kinds of technological learning projects proposed and offered across the curriculum, (b) the stated goals and/or objectives of such programs, (c) the benefits and limitations of the programs, and (d) whether or not reflection and critical thinking skills accompany the learning process in order to encourage understanding of the means through which technology is being deployed. Additionally, this section examines the Massachusetts Department of Education's technology initiatives, district technology planning, and two student learning opportunities, namely the Virtual High School (VHS) project and the Youth Tech Entrepreneurs (YTE) program. By evaluating some recent initiatives to use technology in the classroom, we will be better able to develop arguments about the necessary role of media literacy in cyberspace, which will allow us to identify how "critical autonomy" can best be conceptualized and materialized through tools designed for the Internet-supported classroom.

By designing sample lesson plans aimed at critically evaluating Internet content through the juxtaposition of corporate and noncorporate (profit and nonprofit) Web sites, Chapter 6 illustrates how the development of a curriculum stimulates media literacy in cyberspace. By clarifying our analytic definition of media literacy in relation to current debates about the nature and purpose of media literacy, we will advance the notion that production and critical analysis go hand in hand. This includes both low- and high-tech production elements and is especially important as schools are publishing Web sites that represent their educational philosophies, approaches, and student work, and as students learn to represent themselves through their own Web sites or pages. Without an understanding of the signification of various design elements utilized to produce low- or high-end Web pages with text or graphic capabilities, as well as a proficient understanding of the quality or sources of information contained within their represented text and links, students will once again lose the critical analytical component that I argue must be the thrust of media pedagogy.

Further, as Justin Lewis and Sut Jhally (1998) maintain, media literacy must go beyond a purely "text-centered" approach so that the structure of media institutions are analyzed in order to help Americans appreciate and argue for alternatives to a commercial media system. Accordingly, the design of a cyber-literacy program must center around the political and economic forces that drive much of the Internet. Likewise, we will explore how the Internet presents unique possibilities for nonhegemonic voices, ideas, or representations to emerge through this decentralized technological form. Just as most media literacy programs geared toward traditional print and electronic media (namely television, radio, newspapers, and magazines) argue for the development and awareness of alternatives to commercial productions, we will similarly consider how alternative sources of information can be used to counter mainstream media and can be combined with efforts to inform students of alternative information otherwise absent from mainstream media. Arguments for the possibilities of creative cyber-organizations, forms, and knowledge will require the substitution of Antonio Gramsci's (1971) notion of hegemonic struggle with the concept of domination, pointing to the complex ways in which consent is organized as part of an active pedagogical process within the everyday life. Through a theory of popular culture devised by Henry A. Giroux and Roger Simon (1989), we will explore how the cultural terrain of the Internet is not only a site of struggle and accommodation, but also one in which the production of subjectivity (or interpellation of consumers) can be viewed as a pedagogical process whose structuring principles are deeply political. Likewise, we will examine how the notion of consent, which lies at the heart of the process of hegemony, underscores the importance of specifying the limits and possibilities of the pedagogical principles at work within cyber-cultural forms that serve in contradictory ways to empower and disempower various groups.

Ultimately, the main objective of this book is to enable us to learn to judge the validity and worth of Internet content as we strive to become critically autonomous in a technological world.

## NOTES

1. By "transformative" learning, I am referring to the displacement of traditional power structures within the classroom whereby learning can become a collaborative venture between students and their teachers.

2. Paulo Freire (1989) introduced the notion of the banking metaphor whereby students are encouraged to passively consume the information given to them by their teachers in traditional power-structured classrooms.

Developing
Media Literacy
in Cyberspace

# 1

## Reconceptualizing Learning for the Cyber-Classroom

### COMPUTER TECHNOLOGY AND EDUCATION

Although much scholarship has considered the implications of computer technology in social, political, and economic arenas, critical reflection has predominantly dwelled on the consumption of new programs, software applications, or access to the Internet, both at an individual and an aggregate level, and has focused on the alterations of interpersonal and social interaction through this new medium. Since developments in digitalization and fiber optics technologies are still rapidly unfolding, literature documenting the impact of technologies in education remains on the forefront of an increasingly troublesome sociocultural debate.

In her book *Literacy in a Digital World*, Kathleen Tyner (1998) makes reference to some reviews of literature about the uses of technology for learning. Beginning in 1974, Peggy Campeau published an extensive report funded by the Council of Europe on the way media are selected for specific learning tasks in adult education. While the report sought to find the result of studies on "the instructional effectiveness of media under a variety of learner and treatment conditions" in order to construct a media taxonomy, the results of the literature search revealed less than twelve experimental studies (Campeau, 1974, cited in Tyner, 1998, p. 72). Among the findings, it was discovered that instructional media were used extensively, under many diverse conditions, and that significant funding was spent to install expensive equipment. Interest-

ingly, the report explains that instructional effectiveness has *not* been
the determining criteria for the purchase and use of audiovisual technology. Rather, administrative and organizational considerations of
cost, availability, and user preference have delineated the uses of technology in the classroom. As Campeau explains, this emphasis is not all
that surprising given that current media research in postschool education "has not provided decision makers with practical, valid, depend-
able guidelines for making these choices on the basis of instructional
effectiveness" (cited in Tyner, 1998, p. 72).

With no empirical studies on the effectiveness of learning through
instructional media, Wilbur Schramm entered the scene in 1977, conducting a comprehensive literature review about learning with technology. Schramm assembled empirical applications in a range of media,
including computer-aided education. His findings (1977) offer the following:

> From the experimental studies we have plentiful evidence that
> people learn from the media, but very little evidence as to which
> medium, in a given situation, can bring about the *most* learning.
> We have hints that one medium may be more effective than an-
> other for a given learning task or a given kind of learner, but little
> systematic proof. Thus we can use the media with considerable
> confidence that students will learn from them, but, if we rely only
> on the experimental evidence, not with much discrimination.
> (cited in Tyner, 1998, p. 73)

Since Schramm's study, Tyner (1998) explains that even twenty
years later "there is . . . a dearth of research about the use of digital
technologies in schools" (p. 73). In fact, in 1996 a major study of computer networking conducted by a consortium of federal education and
energy laboratories named Model Nets found "no large-scale studies of
network use in schools that had tested the assumption that computer
networking is a powerful tool that can both help students learn better
and help teachers teach better" (cited in Tyner, 1998, p. 73).

As Tyner confirms, there are few studies that provide accounts of
improved literacy skills through new computer technologies. Tyner is
not alone in her findings. Many scholars and educators in the early
1990s realized that the literacy debates of the 1980s often ignored computers or treated them as obstacles (Tuman, 1992). Myron Tuman explains in *Literacy Online* (1992, p. 3) that we might expect to see in
E. D. Hirsch's *Cultural Literacy* (1987) computer technology as a possible way to provide all Americans with ready access to the knowledge
base about culture that he feels is essential for full literacy. Yet the

single reference to computers offered by Hirsch is not favorable. Caught within an elitist, modernist assumption of culture that privileges some narratives, customs, and behaviors over others, Hirsch believes that "the more computers we have, the more we need shared fairy tales, Greek myths, historical images, and so on" (cited in Tuman, 1992, p. 3). Tuman explains:

> Rather than representing a potential cure for our reading and writing ills, technology in the form of increased specialization is for Hirsch part of the disease, for which the "antidote . . . is to reinvigorate the unspecialized domain of literate discourse." Literacy and technological change are thus opposing cultural forces: "Advancing technology, with its constant need for fast and complex communications, has made literacy more essential to commerce and domestic life." (cited in Tuman, 1992, p. 3)

Unlike Hirsch, authors who situate themselves on the optimistic side of the fence contend that continuing progress in artificial intelligence may well relieve us of many of the traditional burdens entailed in transcribing and decoding texts, simplifying the literacy skills essential for commerce and domestic life (Tuman, 1992, p. 4). Accordingly, computers will reshape not just how we read and write and how these skills are taught, but will alter our very conception of basic terms such as *reading, writing*, and *text*. As Mark Warschauer (1999) explains, celebrants of new electronic literacies claim that they represent much fuller and richer ways to present and access information:

> The decentered, multimedia character of new electronic media facilitates reading and writing processes that are more democratic, learner-centered, holistic, and natural than the processes involved in working with precomputer, linear texts (Bolter, 1991; Lanham, 1993). In their view, hypertext facilitates a critical and dynamic approach to literacy that is an extension of the best traditions of the print world and finally fulfills the visions of critical literacy to reconfigure the text, author, and reader. (Landow, 1992, cited in Warschauer, 1999, pp. 11–12)

New Zealand scholars Lalita Rajasingham and John Tiffin (1995) articulate their vision of education in an information society by radically reconceptualizing the roles of the teacher, the student, pedagogy, and the media. They imagine students using their PCs to both learn and teach themselves through an engagement with multimedia, computer-assisted instruction:

The PC can take on the role of an automated teacher as well as being a source of knowledge and problems . . . the PC will be portable so that the student can work with it anywhere . . . the PC will automatically dial up the virtual educational network and identify itself. Once the system recognizes that it is talking to the PC of a registered student, a menu will appear that allows the student to select from the different kinds of services available in the virtual school or college. . . . These are asynchronous activities, so a student has the flexibility of time as well as space. Electronic libraries and computer-assisted counseling services never close. (p. 120)

Since the "telestudent" will be unrestricted by spatial or temporal dynamics, Rajasingham and Tiffin celebrate the autonomy of the learner through the use of a PC and modem, which allows for independent learning or participation through a virtual class at any time of the day or from any location. Although such a learning environment may increase possibilities for student participation, many questions remain about exactly how critical autonomy can be enabled solely by broader time and spatial parameters.

For educators Ruth Garner and Mark Gillingham (1996), "the educational value for Internet access lies in global community—in McLuhan's [1964] global village" (p. 15). They are less concerned about Neil Postman's (1993) arguments in *Technopoly* that "new technologies are altering society in disturbing ways, that information is dangerous when it has no place to go, when it has no higher purpose, and when there is no theory to which it applies" (p. 16). Garner and Gillingham summarize the praise offered by technological proponents who celebrate the egalitarian nature of the Internet:

Young and old, brainy and not-so-brainy, ugly and handsome persons can participate as long as they have the mechanical tools (computer, account, and telephone access), and each can decide how many personal characteristics to disclose to communication partners. The Internet is not so hierarchical, so attentive to physical shortcomings and social status as, for instance, most high schools that we know. This lack of cliquishness means that Internet participants can learn from and about persons with whom they would have little contact otherwise. (p. 16)

Yet again, as with the celebrated telestudent, access to new communications tools is no guarantee that the means to learning will necessarily lead to fruitful outcomes. Although few doubt that computers change the terrain of communication and education, those situated on the pessimistic side of the fence, or somewhere in between, have provoked considerable debate about the "ubiquity and power of computers in the contemporary world" (Aronowitz, 1992, p. 120). Communication scholar Stanley Aronowitz (1992) summarizes the debates between techno-proponents and opponents, explaining that "enthusiasts consider the computer a *tool*, a term that suggests a neutral social and political content," whereby the "versatility of the computer can provide the key to the historic dream that all work (including schoolwork) can become a vehicle of human creativity, that is, a form of play" (p. 121). Meanwhile, "critics warn that human agency is irreplaceable, that computers cannot do more or less than those who create, program, and operate them" (p. 121). As Warschauer (1999) explains:

> These scholars see net-based reading and writing as fulfilling not the best dreams of critical theory, but the worst nightmares of television, with readers surfing through catchy but vacuous material, never pausing long enough to read something from start to finish, much less critically analyze it. Writing, from such a perspective, would be reduced to searching for the snazziest graphics rather than attending to serious argument. (p. 12)

Despite their optimism for new models of learning, Garner and Gillingham are worried about unequal access to the Internet. Referring to work produced by Tony Scott, Michael Cole, and Martin Engel (1992), they explain that there are inequalities in terms of gender, ethnicity, and class. For example, sons are more likely to have computers purchased for them by their parents than daughters. Moreover, they point out the problem of socioeconomic status, which delimits access to computers and telephone lines. Public libraries, such as those located in New York, are relegated to unequal data-transmission rates, which means they must limit services. This poses inequity among economic status since it means that "middle-class and wealthy children in New York will be part of the information age, and poor children will not— an intolerable situation in a democratic society that espouses the principle of an informed citizenry" (Garner and Gillingham, 1996, p. 17).

Other forms of inequality raised by Garner and Gillingham include reports from the National Center for Education Statistics, which documents that funding is the major barrier to teacher and student Internet access. Citing from Henry Becker's survey data (1995), they explain that

> it generally costs about $86,000 to do electrical work and classroom remodeling necessary to establish the local area network, there are additional one-time costs for Internet connectivity, and there are recurring costs of about $9,000 each year in access fees.

> Poor districts have tremendous difficulty in securing this level of funding without benefactor involvement. This is because schools are funded almost exclusively by a combination of state and local taxpayers. In fact, in what Jonathan Kozol [1991] called "the arcane machinery by which we finance public education" [p. 54], the local property tax is the decisive force in shaping inequality of resources. (Garner and Gillingham, 1996, p. 17)

These issues will undoubtedly impact the future of Internet and computer use in the nation's public schools and inform this study by considering the interconnections between political economy and private business initiatives to provide technology to schools philosophically and materially.[1]

The final concern raised by Garner and Gillingham that deserves mention is their fear that the conservative ideology of vocal network opponents mistakes sexually explicit images on bulletin-board systems with children's classroom Internet communication. This poses another obstacle, as it directly impacts the approval of spending tax dollars to provide Internet access to schools.[2]

Going back to findings by Kathleen Tyner (1998), contemporary studies still produce inconclusive results on the impact of educational technology in enhancing learning. As Tyner explains, since little evidence confirms that student performance is improved by technology, "it is likely that the political call for more digital tools has more to do with issues of social justice and partisan economics than with an expectation in the actual improvement of student gains" (p. 74). She explains that "the quest for broad access to information has a particular cultural resonance in the United States that borders on the mythic":

> The equal access concept resonates with the conventional wisdom that information is the cornerstone of a participatory democracy and a healthy economy. Furthermore, multiliteracies that focus on access to electronic tools, in a technological determinist way, are often aligned with familiar modernist beliefs that equate literacy with progress. (p. 74)

Moreover, the important questions of what to do after schools have technological access are only starting to be asked. As Tyner (1998, p. 74) documents, there is much confusion about the role of technology in the classroom curriculum:

- A 1994 study by the Educational Testing Service (Campbell, Voelke, & Donahue, 1996) found that the uses of computers at home and in school were not clearly tied to focused curricular purposes.

- All students reported that they used the computer mostly to play games (87 percent of K–8 students and 77 percent of high school students).

- They also used the computer to retrieve information "to learn things" (82 percent of K–8 students and 71 percent of high school students) and to write stories or papers (68 percent of fourth-graders, 82 percent of eighth-graders, and 87 percent of eleventh-graders).

- About half of all students surveyed used a computer at home.

Unfortunately, this means that we still know little about the impact and objectives of teaching with new computer-mediated information technologies. However, since the establishment of a curriculum can help identify the learning goals within a particular subject area, we need to come up with effective ways to contribute to sparse research outlining how telecommunications technology can be conceptualized to maximize critical thinking skills and critical autonomy.

## ENVISIONING CRITICAL PEDAGOGY IN CYBERSPACE

Encircled within scholarly debates about the pros and cons of computer and telecommunications technology in schools lies a body of literature, albeit modest in size, that ventures toward the articulation of transformative possibilities within cyberspace. Among the first to conceptualize radical changes for the "virtual class" in the 1990s were Lalita Rajasingham and John Tiffin. In 1995 they articulated their vision of learning in their book *In Search of the Virtual Class*. Rajasingham and Tiffin provide a history of computer-assisted and computer-managed instruction that dates back to the 1960s; telecommunications has been used since the 1970s with audioconferencing, and efforts for instructional television have been going on since the 1950s. However, their vision articulates "the coming together of computer and telecommunications technologies that could lead to the virtual class as the primary locus of learning in society" (p. 5). Through "telelearning," Rajasingham and Tiffin envision the reversal of trends toward big schools especially in the secondary and postsecondary levels, and a return to the village school and small rural college that caters to the neighborhood community. Although city schools have an advantage over small schools by catering to a wide variety of educational needs, "telelearning promises to make it possible to offer a variety of courses that no conventional school could match" (p. 4). Rajasingham and Tiffin explain that the number of courses that can be offered in telelearning is limitless. In fact, they believe it provides new opportunities for the development of a global learning environment whereby individual learners can take classes from teachers in any country on subjects of their choice (pp. 4–5).

Rajasingham and Tiffin are not the only ones who have searched for new paradigms of learning that displace conventional classroom learning and pedagogy. Critical pedagogue Henry Giroux (1996) proposes that educators should become border intellectuals by traveling within and among communities of difference and contends that educational projects need to examine the production and operation of new information systems. Using this as a point of departure, Colin Lankshear, Michael Peters, and Michele Knobel (1996) examine the potential for critical pedagogy to expand and develop within cyberspace environments. They advance several supportive arguments for the utilization of cyberspace to transform classroom practices. First, they contend that cyberspace environments have the potential for making students aware of the historical and contingent nature of discourse. This comes partly as a result of Net users' experiences as creators, refiners, and sustainers of social practices through the act of encoding and decoding symbols and images. Second, interactions, experiences, and information within cyberspace environments point to the complexity, diversity, and multiplicity of human subjectivities, the highly fluid nature of identity, and the enormous possibilities for creating personal identities (all of which challenge modernist notions of subjectivity). Third, conceptualizations of pedagogy can shift from teaching to learning within cyberspace. This results from the fact that, in many instances, students know more about computer-mediated communications technology than do teachers, which displaces traditional power dynamics between educator and educatee. This does not mean that the teacher imparts irrelevant information or knowledge, but that student proficiencies in this area should be tapped into and considered integral aspects of the learning process. Furthermore, students can access a variety of information sources, which allows them to go beyond teacher and textbook knowledge and curriculum details. As a result, learning can potentially become more collaborative between students and teachers. Without giving up claims to authority or valuable information, teachers can deploy knowledge by becoming interrogators, conceptualizers, and facilitators of student-generated questions and ideas.

Lankshear, Peters, and Knobel (1996) go on to explain how critical learning can emerge within cyberspace through three interrelated areas of critical pedagogy, namely information, knowledge, and understanding. Critical pedagogy questions: (1) the nature and role of information within cyberspace environments by problematizing information; (2) how knowledge is legitimated and regulated within cyberspace as it varies from other traditional spaces associated with the book; and (3) how students negotiate which electronically mediated spaces they will join and participate in by making judgments about what forms of information/knowledge make sense to them.

There are many educators who are beginning to realize the importance of combining computer information technologies with school reform. In his foreword to Garner and Gillingham's book *Internet Communications in Six Classrooms* (1996), Bertram Bruce asserts that the purpose, use, and role of e-mail in the classroom must be associated with the teacher's pedagogical goals. For Bruce, a close look at technology, with an emphasis on the Internet, the World Wide Web, e-mail, and virtual communities, brings on the questions of teaching, learning, thinking, communicating, and caring:

> The strengths and weaknesses of computer-mediated communication have little to do with technical features of the new technologies. It is true, of course, that being able to easily share texts across time and space creates possibilities for sharing across cultures that were not afforded previously. But the fascinating exchanges recounted here arose when teachers allowed students to write about things that mattered to them and when teachers worked hard to support students' learning. (p. xii)

Like Lankshear, Peters, and Knobel, Garner and Gillingham (1996) explain that the use of the Internet radically alters the role of the teacher in the classroom. Whereas the teacher usually responds to all speaking and writing assignments, in Internet discourse, writing topics are "chosen by the students, linked to their knowledge and interest rather than to an authorized textbook's contents or a teacher's chalkboard list" (p. 8). Moreover, the Internet allows other students to become the intended audience, rather than the teacher:

> When a topic really appeals, students many miles apart may write back and forth for weeks or even months, negotiating the difficult rhetorical territory of trying to figure out what their distant communication partners know and what more they should say on a variety of topics . . . on an international e-mail list, a handful of students may try to persuade the others of a particular point of view, responding to arguments, point by point, over a series of messages. (p. 9)

As such, the role of the teacher in this lesson is mainly advisory. Garner and Gillingham describe specific classrooms in which the main pedagogy is student-driven learning. They document several instances where the teacher's role as *facilitator* steers the learning process. The first case-in-point entails a fifth-grade teacher in Illinois whose main role in the classroom emerged at the beginning of the year when she introduced the writing revising process by using the overhead projector to have students look for problem areas in structure or mechanics. By the end of the year, most writing revisions took place on the computer as students composed their pieces. The second case is of a high school teacher in Alaska whose students acted as peer editors when writing on the Internet. The third is of a teacher in Philadelphia who shared editing responsibilities with fourth-grade authors, other students, and word-processing tools. Despite the important uses of computers here, the end goal of the writing process has merely been enhanced by the means of technology.

Like Garner and Gillingham, Mark Warschauer (1999) designed and conducted a two-year ethnographic study of the uses of the Internet in four language and writing classrooms in the state of Hawaii. Warschauer believes that at the center of controversies over electronic literacies are broader societal struggles over the nature of literacy and schooling (p. 13). He is equally critical of the technocratic paradigm of literacy that emerged after World War II and continues to dominate in U.S. schools today.[3] While he does not believe that technologies necessitate a particular teaching method or approach, Warschauer believes, like Lankshear, Peters, and Knobel, that computers can be used for a variety of pedagogical purposes depending on the sociocultural context.

Although the body of literature calling for innovative pedagogies is limited, those scholars who do address the subject seem to be in unison in their call for action. As Todd Taylor and Irene Ward (1998) articulate, "to date, not enough effort has been invested in making sure that educational institutions are 'rebuilt' in ways that support effective pedagogy" (p. xvii). Unless computers and the Internet are effectively integrated into the objectives and activities of the classroom teacher, they are unlikely to have a widespread impact on education (Bracey, 1997, p. ix). As Bonnie Bracey (1997), teacher member of the National Information Infrastructure Advisory Council, explains, this means going beyond the use of new equipment by fundamentally transforming their institutional practices. More Web-based lesson plans like those created by Laura Parker Roerden (1997) need to be designed and implemented if teachers are to transform their classroom pedagogy from dispensing all knowledge to serving as a guide. Roerden's development of Web-based instruction for the classroom is unusual because it focuses on curriculum development, asking teachers and administrators to carefully consider how and when the Internet might help them meet their curricular goals. Consequently, further research is needed to document pedagogical innovations designed and utilized by classroom teachers and educational researchers as computer-mediated information technologies emanate in our schools. Once the potential of using Internet resources is realized, teachers can then evolve from "inculcators and deliverers of canned instruction and knowledge to learning facilitators, weaving a tapestry of support to their students" (Falanga, 1996, p. 13).

Accordingly, more thought needs to go into the curriculum development phase of Internet and computer use in the classroom. Despite the broad initiatives we've encountered that are focused on access to communications technology within utopian virtual learning environments, the purpose of exploring cyberspace is obscured if the end goal of the learning venture is overshadowed by the means to get there. Likewise, it is not enough to seek out the destinations of our computer-based quests for knowledge. As educators, administrators, parents, and students, we need to determine why we are undertaking new learning explorations in the first place, establishing the purpose and utility of our excursions so that we know what to do when we get there. The same is true with the production of Internet Web pages. Until we understand why we are creating them and how we can displace top-down models of mass communication through new voices and perspectives, the exciting prospects to be made with this new technology remain thwarted.

## NOTES

1.  Studies demonstrate that school districts with low budgetary funds resort to Channel One's video and editing technology in exchange for broadcasting ads within the classroom. Similarly, computer and Internet access "donations" from the business community to low-income schools will further extend the hand of corporate America in shaping school curricula and advertising products targeted at students.

2.  Garner and Gillingham (1996, p. 19) explain that they attended a Michigan school meeting in which a group of parents mentioned pornography and potential adult e-mail "stalking" of youngsters as reasons to object to spending tax dollars to provide Internet access for their school.

3.  Warschauer explains that a technocratic paradigm views literacy as a series of discrete functional skills that can be taught through isolated technocratic methods that employ a skill-based approach.

# 2

## The Political Economy of Cyber-Media

Although we live in a changing world where telecommunication is reshaping education and learning, transformative possibilities for critical pedagogical practices within cyberspace are not without criticism; analyses of hegemony theory and propaganda models relating to the political economy of the media represent another body of work among media literacy advocates. In an article published by the Center for Media Education (CME) titled "And Now a WEB from Our Sponsor: How Online Advertisers Are Cashing In on Children" (1996), a propaganda model of political economy is the lens through which cyberspace possibilities are conceptualized, since concerns focus on corporate attempts to take advantage of children's vulnerabilities through "virtual playrooms." The threat of potential abuse through the invasive and/or deceptive practices of advertising and market research and the collection of personal information are deemed to be serious impediments to the learning gains offered by the Internet. Whereas Colin Lankshear, Michael Peters, and Michele Knobel (1996) celebrate the displacement of power/ knowledge relations between students and teachers resulting from youth technological know-how, the CME finds the changing relationship of authority between parents and children highly problematic.

An array of similar protestations to advertising on the Internet resound in both mainstream and nonmainstream newspapers. Efforts to have the Federal Trade Commission (FTC) develop safeguards to protect children are articulated within headlines that read, "Cyberseducers? Advertising on the Internet" (DeFalco, 1996), "Snaring Kids in the Net: Firms Use Web to Sell Alcohol, Smokes to Youth" (Cobb, 1997), "Laws Sought for Children's Privacy on Internet" (Dejevsky, 1998) "May Be Unsafe . . . KidsCom Service Draws Data Cops' Scrutiny" (Butterbaugh, 1996), and so forth. Within the articles, the Internet conjures up images of "big, hairy spiders of advertising [that] lurk on the World Wide Web, threatening all the Miss (and Master) Muffets out there" (DeFalco, 1996). Drawing from a report by the Washington, D.C.–based Competitive Enterprise Institute (CME), policy analyst Julie DeFalco (1996) explains that Internet sites are being accused of enlisting the sponsorship of various manufacturers of kid-oriented products such as breakfast cereal and toys, manufacturers that are not just new places to advertise goods but that are also using " 'highly manipulative forms of advertising, often disguised as information or entertainment, which could intrude into every corner of the lives of children.' "

As described by the *The Independent* (London, 1998), the FTC surveyed 1,400 commercial Internet sites and found that only 14 percent gave any indication of how the personal information they collected would be used, let alone any guarantee that the information would not be passed to third parties. The report cited several companies operating "chat rooms" for children, which requested full name, address, e-mail address, and hobbies, thereby allowing the children to be easily tracked and targeted by advertisers (Dejevsky, 1998). In response to growing concerns about "familiar cartoon characters prancing around World Wide Web sites and inviting children to enter contests, buy products or provide information about themselves," the *New York Times* described how one advertising industry group decided to release new voluntary guidelines for " 'responsible marketing to children' " on the Internet (Mifflin, 1997). The guidelines provided by the Children's Advertising Review Unit (CARU) build upon those used by the industry for twenty-three years to help regulate media advertising targeted at children. Among the guidelines, advertisers are encouraged to make "reasonable efforts" to have children get their parents' permission before buying a product or service through the Internet or before disclosing personal information about themselves or their families. If children are asked to disclose information, advertisers are asked to state why they are asking for it and how it will be used (e.g., "We'll e-mail you with information," or "You'll be added to our mailing list"). According to the 1996 study cited within the *Times* article, about four million children under age eighteen regularly use the Internet, which is two million more than the year prior.[1]

*New York Times* writer Lawrie Mifflin (1997) describes the strategies used by corporate Web sites aimed at children:

At the McDonald's Web site, for example, children are invited to write to Ronald McDonald and tell him their name, grade in school, favorite McDonald's food item and favorite sport, and they get an E-mail response if they do so. . . . M&M's Web site does not collect information from children, but it does attempt to get them to stay for an extended period, using interactive material. In one humorous instance, for example, the M&M cartoon characters are screen testing for a movie version of "Hamlet." Rather than trying specifically to sell the product, the site aims to build brand loyalty. . . . Coca-Cola's Web site is aimed at preteens who are interested in activities like skateboarding—and in slaking their thirsts with soft drinks. To gain access to the site, users must register, with a log-on and identification. This lets Coca-Cola send back a message reminding the user of those bits of information—presumably, so that the site can be visited again.

Although the vice president and director of the Children's Advertising Review Unit, Elizabeth Lascoutx, is cited as being "optimistic that regulatory guidelines will be as successful with the new media as they have been with the old," former FTC member Christine A. Varney isn't sure whether a regulatory code needs to emerge or whether it can be voluntary (Mifflin, 1997). But as CME president Kathryn C. Montgomery forewarns, "we should err on the side of caution, of protection of children" (Mifflin, 1997).

Criticism of Internet advertising is not limited to kid-oriented products. Seth Schiesel (1997) of the *New York Times* documents that "children's advocates and public health officials are becoming increasingly concerned that liquor and beer companies and, to a lesser extent, tobacco companies are turning their marketing muscle to cyberspace." Detailing some questionable Web sites, Schiesel presents some of the "characters lurking" within cyberspace:

Take J.C. Roadhog, the cartoonish rodent star of an on-line game who races through a desert littered with empty tequila bottles bearing the label of Cuervo Especial, the sponsor of the game on the brand's World Wide Web site. Visitors to an Anheuser-Busch, Inc. Web site called "The Pad" meet the three frogs from Budweiser's television commercials, including Budbrew J. Budfrog, whose biography reveals that he was elected president of his college fraternity and that he "likes to land on the beach with a hot babe, a cold Bud and a folio edition of the Kama Sutra in its original Sanskrit." Absolut vodka's home page on the Web features video clips of the Absolut bottle in witty disguises. The print versions of Absolut ads have become collector's items among some children.

As Schiesel explains, the problem with such cyber-ads is that they target and reach youth under the legal drinking age who are especially vulnerable to slick Internet pitches that combine games, online chat forums, and other entertainment forms with messages touting drinking and smoking.

These articles indirectly refer to the conundrum that schools face regarding the use of technology in schools. In an article that examines the political and economic forces driving the use of television, video, and computers in schools, Erik Strommen (1995) asks the essential question, "who pays the freight?":

> Whether the digital future comes slow or fast, though, educators will always be looking for video with good content and an affordable price tag. However, as production costs go up and school budgets go down, educational programming is increasingly being provided by media companies not education organizations. Increasingly, schools are becoming places where businesses—cable companies, software manufacturers, broadcasters—make the decisions about educational content because they are the ones producing it. Ironically, just as teachers are mastering video as a tool, she [Mary Lou Ray, vice president for learning services at the Pacific Mountain Network a PBS affiliate] says "they end up having more control over how learning occurs but less control over what is learned."

Despite the legitimacy and seriousness of such stated concerns, others have been quick to note that such perceived "threats" of "child safety" are ill founded. Julie DeFalco (1996) rebuts accusations about online marketing and advertising to children by stating that no evidence of damage has been produced by the CME report. She explains that the report "merely asserts that 'a number of marketing and advertising practices . . . are potentially harmful to children,'" and is vague on the details of just how these " 'new forms of manipulation and exploitation are really new.'" DeFalco quips that "web sites are simply a new generation of advertising, and contrary to the CME's fears, they are actually less intrusive than are television and print ads." Yet she does not explain *how* they are less invasive. Not surprisingly, her tone parallels the business community's response to the benignity of advertising, implying that, like television and radio, you can simply turn away from or avoid advertising if you are offended or feel threatened by it:

> Some children's activity pages do have links to advertising sites, but they are labeled and easy to avoid. For example, one play page is sponsored by Microsoft. A bar at the top of the page says so. When you click on it, you go to Microsoft's children's page. If you don't like it, you click back to the original page. This exercise is only a problem if you are worried that Microsoft might "have activities designed to keep children engaged for extended periods of time," that is, that Microsoft might entertain your kids. At any rate, in many cases a child would have to type in the Web address of a particular company's Web site to even get to the "incessant hucksterism" that the CME laments.

Unfortunately, DeFalco's resolution of clicking back to the original page represents an *individual* (quasi)solution to indignation over advertised links rather than a systematic critique of advertising's sociopolitical consequences. DeFalco trivializes the concerns recounted by the CME, stating that since no actual harm can be pointed to, the report "resorts to scare tactics that range from obvious to silly." She pokes fun at concerns that children's online areas are quickly being populated by a growing number of animated characters and products designed to develop relationships with children that will foster brand loyalty.

Shelly Pasnik, coauthor of the CME report, elaborates that if a child sees an ad on the Net for a product he wants, asks his mother for it, and she says no, then "the company has driven a wedge between the parent and the child. The parent now looks like the bad guy" (CME report, cited in DeFalco, 1996). Without any regard for advertisers' cultivation of consumer desire, DeFalco responds, "that's not a marketing problem; it's a parenting problem." For DeFalco:

> Advertising's purposes in a market economy are essential, and essentially benign: informing potential consumers of the existence and price of products, both new and old. Since children rarely control their own disposable income, the dangers of having their decisions manipulated by advertising are even less than for adults. And despite the psychology and communications research the CME uses to bolster its assertions, according to one advertising expert, the bulk of serious advertising and marketing literature demonstrates that as children age, they are increasingly skeptical about advertising.

Once again, DeFalco does not consider the fact that the majority of advertisements provide neither the price of products nor relevant information regarding the product purpose or function. Furthermore, although children may be skeptical or even cynical about advertising, that cynicism does not translate into immunity from product loyalty, critical action, or resistance of cultural consumption. DeFalco does not see the association between the children's advertising and the determination of the family's disposable income. Primary colors, free toys in Happy Meals, playground equipment, and clown Ronald McDonald would prove to be poor advertising strategies for McDonald's fast-food chains if children had no impact on family spending.

In addition to advertising, DeFalco continues her rebuke of the concerns raised by the CME, downplaying the significance of privacy policies: "If anti-advertising hysteria isn't enough to make the FTC dance to the CME's tune, it has a backup alarm to sound: privacy." DeFalco is referring to the report's statement that a growing number of children's areas are now eliciting personal information, some of which include the use of incentives like free gifts in exchange for such personal data as e-mail addresses. DeFalco believes that companies are following an old tradition in soliciting names, addresses, and other consumer information on the Internet. Far from critiquing such marketing ploys, she defends, "for decades, children have sent in cereal box tops—and their addresses—to get magic decoder rings and other sundries." Like many who see only within a market-driven Internet system, DeFalco concludes by suggesting that rather than regulating the Internet environment, parents should purchase inexpensive software such as NetNanny, which can prevent children from releasing any personal information. She believes that without ads, choices of sites would be limited to government-funded sites.

Although not all defenders of the Internet are pro-advertising, there are those who argue that "virtual spaces" are safer than most school, playground, and street environments. As Stephen Collins explains in "Web66: A Fear of Rare and Mysterious Dangers" (1997), parents are pleased when their students are recognized for their academic achievements in traditional media forms, such as newspapers, television, and radio, but they panic when their children's names are included on the Internet. Yet, as he explains, perceived threats of "child safety" on the Internet can be compared with media exaggerations about the dangers of flying, child pornography, and kidnapping.

Likewise, Nicholas Burbules (in "Misinformation, Malinformation, Messed-Up Information, and Mostly Useless Information: How to Avoid Getting Tangled Up in the Net" [forthcoming] contends that the alarms and fears over bomb-building, neo-Nazi group activity, and finding naked pictures of children through the Internet as presented through media sensationalism fail to make the point that such information can be obtained through well-stocked bookstores and libraries. Of course, this information is more easily accessible electronically, suggesting that the Internet provides some advantages over other traditional resources. Nevertheless, Burbules believes that much of the sensationalism about the Internet among the news media is a result of the media's own discomfort with, and perceived threat of, such technology as it affects their practice.

While Collins and Burbules are certainly justified in identifying and problematizing the hype that typically accompanies new technological innovations, they represent and address only some of the troubling elements of the Internet previously mentioned. Nevertheless, Burbules goes further to suggest strategies that concerned parents, educators, and administrators can use. In devising methods to overcome "Internet paranoia," Burbules explains three procedures that can be taken on the part of concerned groups (including educators). First, as DeFalco suggests, screening software can be purchased so that categories of material/information can be blocked from the point of reception. Many schools have made such purchases in order to control the types of information students can access. However, this poses several problems for critical learning and research projects (e.g., the difficulties posed when a student wants to access information on the Net for a report on "breast cancer" or "sex education," in which case information from the categories of "breast" and "sex" is restricted). Another approach is information censorship, in which parties/groups advocate the central regulation of certain kinds of material on the Net. However, the problem with such regulation is that many groups attempt to censor material (under the guise of concerns for "child safety") that poses a threat to their own political and/or religious aims.

Contrary to these restrictive strategies, Burbules contends that a much better approach toward new information technologies is to go beyond teaching students about how to use computers, e-mail, Web browsers, and so forth. As I will articulate, the goals of media literacy need to go hand in hand with computer training through the instruction of critical skills by which students learn to discriminate "misinformation, malinformation, messed-up information, and mostly useless information" (Burbules). While there are hazards to overregulation and underregulation of the Internet, Burbules explains that there will always be an overabundance of junk on the Net. Consequently, it makes more sense to teach students to become discerners of the types of information they need so that they can access, evaluate, and effectively use the information they desire. As students become more experienced with new technologies, they can come up with their own strategies for finding and evaluating information. My arguments for a cyber-media literacy go further, emphasizing not only the critical evaluation and use of information, but also an understanding of the political and economic forces that drive and control much of the Internet.

Lankshear, Peters, and Knobel similarly articulate how cyberspace possibilities are associated with media literacy goals. Contrary to the traditional limits of newspaper space and broadcast airtime, the Internet offers unrestricted space through the broad expansion of information/topics that can be accessed. Unlike traditional analyses of media, which focus on the limits of active audience participation (or production) within televisual and print media, the Internet allows for interactive discourses to emerge within and across diverse communities so that recipients are no longer "passive," but can question, react, and respond through interactive communication.

Hence, as each of the three bodies of literature outlined above indicates, there are many benefits that emerge from the fusion of media literacy, critical pedagogy, and cyberspace. Yet, as this study will elucidate, the objectives and goals of media literacy will need to be broadened to include the critical analysis of computer-mediated communications technology. A careful balance must be achieved between cyberspace pessimists and optimists. As David Shaefer explains in *Media Literacy in the Communication Age* (1995), traditional media literacy approaches neglect the human-to-human interactions that emerge from multimedia technologies by focusing on teaching (a) passive audiences to become critical, and (b) "would-be" producers how to efficiently operate technical equipment. Despite the importance of learning such consumption/production skills, Shaefer argues that such approaches reify the "information age" assumption of the "thingness" of technology itself, which fails to account for how end-users of technology are active participants in the co-production/negotiation of meaning. As Jurgen Habermas (1989) proposes through his model of the critical public sphere, Shaefer contends that media literacy should focus on communicative consciousness—how to understand and be understood by others within virtual communities. Accordingly, the goals of media literacy should be grounded within a dialogic approach focused on teaching media users the ability to evaluate and produce multimedia content; the ability to critically evaluate the political and economic systems that produce, regulate, and distribute multimedia technologies; and finally, the ability to communicate effectively with other users of multimedia technology (to understand and be understood by others, even if this means acknowledging that effective communication has not occurred) (Shaefer).

In effect, although there is no consensus among educators that information literacy, media literacy, and/or critical literacy are the essential foundations for learning, combinations of all three can inform new learning paradigms that neither fully embrace technology nor discount the potential for cyber-literacy in an age of information.

## NOTE

1. The study was conducted by Jupiter Communications, a New York media research firm that tracks computer use.

# 3

## Moving Beyond Literacy Theory

### THE BUILDING BLOCKS OF MEDIA LITERACY

If we are going to adopt an appropriate model for learning excursions in cyberspace, we need to carefully examine the basic elements that make *media* literacy different from traditional literacy theory. Although the word *literacy* is not limited to one meaning, it describes the process of learning to read and write using language associated with print-based texts or alphabetic components. Synonymous with literacy are the terms *literature, literary*, and *literate*, all of which describe the extent of one's reading proficiency through written language. Oftentimes, literacy connotes a highbrow application of language so that it directly relates to one's level of education, familiarity with literature, and ability to write "polite," "proper," and/or "polished" essays. Those marked as "literate" are well read in what usually consists of selected canonical works of literature.

Due to the fact that literacy requires an understanding of the grammar, structure, mechanics, and playful usage of language, the process of "decoding" or interpreting the messages in a given text depends on one's comprehension of how language is organized, which oftentimes is arranged in imaginative and unusual ways. Literary criticism has entailed a variety of approaches, such as understanding how a literary text functions, the effectiveness of the text in conveying ideas and values, both old and new, the capacity of the text to represent "reality" as associated with notions of "Truth," and the interrelationships between the text and the author's intent. Yet such approaches have been dismantled by new shifts in thinking that understand that the function and purpose of a text is contextual, historical, cultural, and personal. Moreover, "Truth" is not "out there" but is contingent on ideology and point of view inasmuch as "reality" is socially constructed. Thus the attempt to discover the author's underlying intent for a text is daunting and perhaps not as important as examining the effect or response evoked by the text.

When combining literacy with media, we begin to shift from a print-based literary sphere to a visual world whereby cultural texts are composed of a host of nonlinear signs and symbols that create meaning. Unlike the elite posturing of literacy within a privileged culture, the terrain of the popular is a crucial site of exploration and creativity so that the mediated "texts" that emerge from within the everyday are subject to critical analysis. The reason why *media* literacy is vital for today's generation has to do with the increasing deluge of visual, auditory, and multimedia messages that we're exposed to, from television programs and commercials, to newspaper stories, billboards, radio announcements, sales catalogs, and information acquired from the Internet. Although literacy requires an engagement with a text in order to grapple with meaning, more often than not, the messages within multimedia are accepted without stopping to question and/or examine the ideas, values, or motives behind these messages and their producers. Inasmuch as the "intent" or "meaning" of the text is a focal point of literacy, comprehending the function and effect of a given visual text remains essential to media literacy.

At the heart of a media literacy criticism is both a personal and a sociocultural engagement with multimedia. Criticism has been known to emphasize one's negative disposition in relation to a text; however *media* criticism involves an evaluation of our love/hate relationship with the media: for instance, we might enjoy specific television programs or magazines, but become annoyed with commercials or ads that suggest women must be extremely thin to be beautiful or must determine their success through stereotypical ideals. Although most of us are media savvy, it is important to go beyond cynicism and skepticism by becoming critical consumers of informative and persuasive media messages.[1] We must also become critically engaged citizens.[2] When using the term *critical*, we're referring to the process of keeping a watchful eye on the mass media by using learned media literacy skills to detect bias, biased representations, inaccurate statements and falsities, and/or the value messages of a text. Media "texts" include not only print forms of communication, but also broadcast and electronic media such as films, television, computer software products, and the like.

As officially defined in most national and international contexts, media literacy is the ability to (1) "read" media texts by analyzing, accessing, and evaluating communication in a variety of forms, and (2) "write" media texts by producing messages through personal experience, narrative, and point of view. By learning to critically "read" and "write" media, we can become an effective informed citizenry, making better choices and acting in the best interest of ourselves and others.

Before further discussing the "literacy" aspect of media literacy, it is important that we understand what we mean by "media." Media are vehicles that convey messages. There are print texts, such as newspapers, magazines, books, and catalogs; visual texts, such as television, movies, computers, billboards, and performing arts; audio texts, such as music and radio; and multimedia, such as computers, the World Wide Web, and the Internet. Most media messages use a combination of forms. For instance, television and movies use still and moving images, sound effects, and music. A person's individual style also sends a message. Body language, dress, makeup, hairstyle, tone of voice, and facial expressions convey meaning nonverbally. Thus there are many ways to send messages.

When we talk about the "mass media," we're referring to those industries and companies whereby control of the production and distribution of messages lies in the hands of a small number of individuals. Those messages are then disseminated to large masses of people. Newspapers and magazines are examples of print mass media. Television, radio, DVDs, video games, and online computer services are examples of electronic mass media.

Mass media have a powerful place and serve an important role in a democracy. The public's vision of the world, society, and self is shaped by words and images projected by the mass media. Much of the information we get about public business comes from mass media sources. Nevertheless, the exercise of democracy is affected by the constraints on mass media organizations.[3] High production costs, advertising, and deadlines are just some of the components that affect media content. Since most print and electronic mass media are supported primarily from advertising, sponsors of a particular show or event can withdraw their support if they find the content displeasing. For instance, sponsors have pulled their advertisements from television episodes of *Ellen* or *Roseanne* because they dealt with homosexual issues. Moreover, programs with low ratings have a difficult time attracting individual sponsors. Shows that have displayed strong female role models, such as *Grace Under Fire*, or intelligent female news anchors such as Connie Chung, have lost support from advertisers as a result of low ratings, or high ratings with the "wrong" demographic group (i.e., older, moderate-to low-income viewers). Likewise, newspapers and magazines need to maintain a high circulation to attract advertisers, and increasingly they need to be able to target their deliveries to particular segments of their subscriber lists in order to satisfy customers. Thus magazines such as *Seventeen* and *Elle* aim to attract young adolescent women through their advertisements and feature stories.

There are eight key media literacy concepts used by most media literacy educators and advocacy groups.[4] These concepts are the result of many efforts to focus, narrow, and define the scope of media literacy since the 1980s. One of the overarching premises of media literacy is that reality is socially constructed. Accordingly, the first tenet of media literacy is that *all media are constructions*. Even though the media appear to be merely reflecting the world, they are carefully created through multimedia effects. With increased technological sophistication, the "seams" of most media texts are rendered invisible, making it difficult for us to see the media as manufacturers of reality, or manipulators of common sense. Our task, then, is to make visible the seams of the media that otherwise go unnoticed in our everyday lives.

The second principle of media literacy is that *the media construct reality* (reality is socially constructed). We discussed how literary theory has involved a preoccupation with the discovery of "Truth" as an enlightened intellectual process. Yet we now know that truth is not transcended, but is created in our daily lives. The ways in which we come to understand how society functions and how we fit into society are based on our familial upbringing, schooling, and religion, as well as on our growing up in a certain community, region, and nation. Thus our ideas, values, and belief system—ideology—are formed from material conditions and our situatedness in the world. Like other institutional and sociocultural structures, the media provide us with certain viewpoints, opinions, and explanations of how the world works. Due to the fact that we're spending more and more time consuming media in all forms, we must carefully examine the media's influential role in packaging reality.

While the media construct reality, we do not necessarily see, experience, or relate to the same reality as the one projected in the media. Hence the third factor is that *audiences negotiate meaning in media* (audience analysis). Even though we all consume and engage with media, we don't all have the same experiences or interpretations. Our individual pleasures, desires, and fears will affect our understanding of media messages, as will our levels of education, gender, age, race, ethnicity, and sexuality. It makes sense, then, that no two people will interpret a given message in exactly the same way. Differences in gender and generation can lead to varied aesthetic pleasures and interpretations of musical genres, soap operas, sports, computer games, and films, depending on what experiences, values, and belief systems we bring to these "texts." Put simply, meaning is "negotiated" in multiple ways.

Expanding on earlier statements, the fourth principle refers to the commercial implications of the media. It is not enough to examine the meaning that emerges from a given form of media, as its meaning is contingent upon its economic function. Consequently, media literacy involves an awareness and understanding of the interrelationships between the financial underwriting of production in the mass media and its resulting content, techniques, and distribution. Also known as *political economy*, we need to acknowledge that the mass media are part of a profit-making business, and as such are deeply political. For instance, the television industry uses audience ratings as a means to assess all programs—news, public affairs, or entertainment. Even an audience of twenty million viewers isn't large enough for most television shows to be kept on the air. In addition to the number of viewers, the demographic composition of audiences for certain media forms is vital in determining the "merits" of a given show or medium for advertisers. Thus media literacy requires a basic understanding of how audiences are divided into marketable groups and "sold" to advertisers seeking to profit from program content.

In addition to addressing advertising, we also need to examine the impact of corporate ownership of the media. Over the course of the last twenty years, large multi–billion dollar global conglomerates have emerged as powerful monopolies controlling both the production and the distribution of media. With fewer independently owned and operated media companies, there lacks a diversity in the types of media produced and disseminated to the public. Thus decisions to produce and not produce certain books, magazines, television shows, movies, music, and computer games rest in the hands of a few powerful groups. One serious effect of the concentration of ownership of the media can be seen in the newspaper industry. Whereas more than 60 percent of U.S. cities had two or more competing newspapers in 1923, the number is now down to 2 percent. Naturally, the point of view and story selection in news reporting are directly affected by the economic organization of the media.

The fifth element of media literacy is that *media contain ideological and value messages*. We need to acknowledge that the media are disseminators of ideological material, and that they thereby promote some value and belief systems over others. More often than not, the media espouse belief systems that reinforce the existing social structure. As such, ideas prevalent within dominant social structures—the business community, government, schools, religion—are strengthened within the media. Certain ways of life are explicitly and implicitly promoted in the media. This includes American ideologies that value freedom as an individual rather than social right, buying products as a way to gain happiness and success, competing with others to get ahead, affirming nationalistic superiority, reinforcing differences across lines of race, class, and gender, and adhering to authority. Like fish in water, these basic ideologies are rendered invisible to us as Americans, until we find ourselves in new cultural surroundings or contexts. Media literacy requires that we challenge ourselves to continually think "outside the box"—the television box, film screen, radio box, and computer box—so that we can take apart the basic ideological messages and value systems of our society.

In addition to reflecting the social needs and goals of powerful individuals, groups, a class, or a culture, *media have social and political implications* (cultivation analysis).[5] Accordingly, the sixth dimension of media literacy is an awareness of the broad range of social and political effects stemming from the media. For instance, television viewing has directly affected the nature of family life by replacing interactive family activities with inactive and isolated media consumption. Moreover, the media have directly impacted the use of leisure time in that people watch, on average, about four hours of television a day, while the television set is on for approximately seven hours in the average household. We could certainly argue about the extent of the media's role in creating values and ideas. But rather than identifying whether or not the media are the ultimate determiners of social thought, we need to explore how the media legitimize and reinforce some ideologies over others. Shopping, for instance, has become the new national pastime in the United States, precisely at a time when the glut of advertised products in the media has reached a saturation point. In addition to affecting our use of leisure time, the media affect our understandings of ourselves and others by grouping us according to the consumption choices we make. Thus the media not only define our relationship to popular culture, but they also inform us of who we are in relationship to our peers.

In a larger context, the media today are closely linked with the world of politics and social change (action). Because of television, we are much more likely to vote for our national leaders based on images and soundbites over policies and issues. Likewise, our exposure to politics is increased as we receive late-breaking news from local protests to international crises halfway across the world. Ironically, while we may feel more directly aware of certain political goings-on, we are often dependent on the media to tell us how we are supposed to interpret and react to political events, which usually involves sitting on the sidelines as spectators rather than directly playing in the "game."

The two final tenets of media literacy are that *form and content are closely related in the media*, and each medium has a unique aesthetic form. Canadian scholar Marshall McLuhan (1964) argued that each medium has its own grammar and classifies reality in unique ways. Consequently, even though various media will cover the same stories or events, our experiences, engagements, and interpretations of these events are directly related to the media form. To hear a ball game broadcast on the radio provides us with a uniquely different experience from watching it on television, as we have to use our imagination to make up for the lack of visuals present.

Unlike high and low cultural distinctions that may polarize the worthiness of literary works, media literacy is predicated on the assumption that we can enjoy as well as understand the different aesthetic forms of media texts. To "critically engage" with the media does not mean that one must take a negative oppositional stance toward all media. Rather, media literacy leads to a more complete appreciation and understanding of how meanings are produced and enhanced through media production.

Once we have applied all of these concepts through theory and practice, our ability to become critical consumers of all media is rendered possible. Accordingly, this process "enables us to establish and maintain the kind of critical distance within our culture that makes possible critical autonomy: the ability to decode, encode, evaluate, and (re)act upon the symbol systems that dominate our world" (*Media Literacy Resource Guide*, 1989).

## THE GOALS AND APPROACHES OF MEDIA LITERACY

Having examined the basic elements of media literacy, we need to clarify some of the commonly used terms and objectives within media literacy. In *Teaching the Media* (1985), British scholar Len Masterman stresses that the primary goal of media education is not to have students regurgitate the ideas, critical perspectives, or knowledge provided by the teacher. Nor should it simply encourage students to develop their own critical propensities. For Masterman, "the really important and difficult task of the media teacher is to develop in pupils enough self-confidence and critical maturity to be able to apply critical judgements to media texts *which they will encounter in the future*":

The acid test of any media education programme is the extent to which pupils are critical in their own use and understanding of the media *when the teacher is not there*. The primary objective is not simply critical awareness and understanding, it is critical *autonomy*. (pp. 24–25)

This notion of critical autonomy is essential to media education if only in the fact that it stresses the importance of having a student-driven pedagogy that encourages learning beyond classroom walls and beyond the K–12 learning years. According to Masterman, a media pedagogy means that nonhierarchical teaching methods promoting reflection and critical thinking must be accompanied by lively, democratic, group-focused, and action-oriented teaching (p. 27).[6] Hence it is the teacher's responsibility to use pedagogical approaches that help students gain confidence through group dialogue, and in which students can make their own judgments, develop the ability to analyze those judgments, and take on the responsibility for their own learning, thinking, and action (p. 28). Despite the meritable intentions of both pedagogical initiatives, I will be questioning the viability and embedded assumptions within these strategies for critical learning in the next section on critical pedagogy.

While many media educators and advocates understand and reference the principal tenets of media literacy, this is not to suggest that there is a general consensus about the movement's goals. Rather than providing Masterman's emphasis on critical autonomy, there are some media education programs that focus on providing students with marketable skills that will enable them to find jobs as future media workers, uncritical of current media structures or practices. As David Sholle and Stan Denski (1994) explain, the practice of video, audio, photography, and graphics media in the United States is usually situated within *schooling* programs aimed at offering skill enhancement and/or career development. Other schooling initiatives encourage students to creatively express themselves through new media forms and aesthetic experimentation without a critical understanding of media systems. This has led to several debates between disjointed factions of primary and secondary school educators, academics, media artists, and media executives.

Most debates centered around the objectives of media education are divided over the balance between media analysis and production. As Deborah Leveranz and Kathleen Tyner (1993) explain, those favoring analysis believe that production is only important if it helps students understand how to analyze mass media products. Proponents of media analysis are typically school teachers and university educators who believe in a formal, structured approach to media education. Not surprisingly, many of these teachers have no training in production and are often not particularly comfortable with media technologies.

Production advocates are typically media artists who have observed the "power of student production to increase student self-esteem through self-expression and to offer a voice to those who have been marginalized by mass media" (Leveranz & Tyner, 1993, p. 23). Media artists believe that a hands-on approach is the best way to teach the analytical component. Moreover, many have witnessed the demise of the arts in public education institutions and believe that media arts education can strengthen the arts.

Needless to say, the debates polarizing analysis and production are only part of the contentious circumstances surrounding media education. Although not all of the debates will be outlined in the purview of this study, a brief summary of some conceptual and application issues as outlined in the 1998 (Winter) *Journal of Communication* edition on media literacy is useful in understanding the complexity of the subject. Scholars William Christ and W. James Potter (1998, p. 7) explain that defining media literacy poses the central conceptual debate. Media literacy has been treated as

- a public policy issue (Aufderheide, 1993),
- a critical cultural issue (Alvarado & Boyd-Barrett, 1992),
- a set of pedagogical tools for elementary school teachers (Houk & Bogart, 1974),
- suggestions for parents (DeGaetano & Bander, 1996; Kelly, 1983),
- McLuhanesque speculation (Gordon, 1971), and
- a topic of scholarly inquiry from a physiological (Messaris, 1994), cognitive (Sinatra, 1986), or anthropological (Scribner & Cole, 1981) tradition.

Some writers focus on several countries or cultures (Bazalgette, Bevort, & Savino, 1992; Brown, 1991; Maddison, 1971; Scheunemann, 1996), while others focus primarily on one culture, such as

- American culture (Manley-Casimer & Luke, 1987; Ploghoft & Anderson, 1981),
- British culture (Buckingham, 1990; Masterman, 1985), and
- Chilean culture (Freire, 1985).

It is a term applied to the study of

- textual interpretation (Buckingham, 1998; Messaris, 1998; & Meyrowitz, 1998; Zettl, 1998),
- context and ideology (Lewis & Jhally, 1998), and
- audience (Buckingham, 1998, cited in Christ & Potter, 1998)

The term is also used as synonymous with, or part of, *media education* (Sholle & Denski, 1994).

Moreover, in the Winter 1998 issue of the *Journal of Communication*, Renée Hobbs and David Buckingham explain how the terms *media* and *literacy* both present controversy. In contesting the term *media*, academics, teachers, and parents wonder which medium should be the focus of study (i.e., oral and written versus still and moving images, computers, or multimedia); regarding the notion of *literacy* are questions that ask: How broadly should literacy be conceptualized? Should it be regarded primarily as a skill, as an accumulation of knowledge, or as a perspective on the world? (Hobbs, 1998; Buckingham, 1998, cited in Christ & Potter, 1998, p. 7)

The final conceptual issues I will mention concern the divergent educational models espoused through media literacy. As Christ and Potter summarize:

> The two main theoretical views of media literacy, inoculation theory and cultural studies, bring with them orientations toward the subject matter and assumptions about the audience that impact not only interpretation but how the subject matter is taught. (Buckingham and Kubey, cited in Christ & Potter, 1998, p. 8)

As Buckingham (1998) explains, inoculation theory emerged from the work of literary critic F. R. Leavis and his student Denys Thompson (1933). In their book *Culture and Environment*, Leavis and Thompson offered a framework for the teaching of mass media in schools. Yet their impetus was driven by cultural elitism and the conservation of a "distinguished literary heritage." For Leavis and Thompson, teaching about popular culture was not a radical pedagogical discovery, but a method of teaching students to learn to inoculate or defend themselves from the invasion of the corrupting influence of mass media.

While inoculation theory informs a pedagogical model that empowers *individuals* (Messaris, 1998; Hobbs, 1998), cultural studies stresses the capability of media literacy to transform *society* (Lewis & Jhally, 1998). As I will be articulating in the next section, I believe that both approaches deserve consideration. However, I will be problematizing the underlying assumptions within cultural studies that "democratic" possibilities are inherently commendable and achievable.

## CRITICAL PEDAGOGY

In his foreword "Critical Theory and the Meaning of Hope" (1988), Peter McLaren contends that the goals of critical pedagogy are "to empower students to intervene in their own self-formation and to transform the oppressive features of the wider society to make such an intervention necessary" (p. xi). Contrary to the banking metaphor, in which it is the teacher's task to deposit knowledge into "empty" students (Freire, 1989), McLaren asks: Do we want our schools to create a passive, risk-free citizenry, or a political citizenry committed to forms of public life and invested in advancing social and political equality?

In *Media Education and the (Re)Production of Culture* (1994), David Sholle and Stan Denski argue that critical pedagogy is about more than "teaching techniques." Rather, critical pedagogy is about the analysis of those processes that define what knowledge is important to know, how we should learn it, and how the production of knowledge creates social identity. Similarly, Henry Giroux and Roger Simon (1989) suggest that "any process which tries to influence the production of meaning is a pedagogical process" (p. 230). Thus the pedagogical can occur outside schools and within the family, public discourse, the church, the media, and so forth (Sholle and Denski 1994, p. 23).

Despite the importance of the aforementioned definitions of critical pedagogy, critical pedagogues need to acknowledge the fundamental tension between a theory/pedagogy that on the one hand calls for a liberatory democratic classroom (a safe space where true participation can occur), and on the other hand views schooling as the institutionalization of dominant ideologies and cultural production (where teacher-as-critic is the primary role). Accordingly, we will explore a critical pedagogy of risk and articulation rather than a progressive pedagogy of emancipation and democratic participation. This will serve as the cornerstone of the pedagogical infrastructure outlined in the subsequent chapters.

In contesting modernist conceptions of "equality," "social justice," "democracy," and "emancipation," we find ourselves in accordance with critical pedagogues whose philosophical pedagogical approaches are advanced through postmodernism. In *Issues and Trends in Critical Pedagogy* (1997), Barry Kanpol argues that critical pedagogy should be situated within a critical postmodernism that questions those worldviews that uphold and perpetuate "absolutes" and "universal truths." As critical pedagogues, we need to ask, accordingly: Whose knowledge or worldviews are we teaching? How is identity constructed? How many ways of learning are there? How many realities are there?

Moreover, Kanpol argues that a critical postmodernism is politically aligned with unraveling the processes that define social, cultural, and human difference, with an eye toward a shift of consciousness to challenging and transforming unequal relations of power and overcoming oppression, subordination, and alienation. Such goals are commensurate with Paulo Freire's work (1989), in which oppressed people can undertake to transform their lives by understanding those structures of power that set them up as unequal members of society.

One of the lauded goals of critical pedagogy has been its concern for diversity, multiculturalism, and democracy. Yet again there are many issues to be raised in light of the ways critical pedagogues and media literacy advocates have theorized these concepts. First, as Kanpol argues, critical pedagogy should foster a critical multiculturalism founded in understanding "difference" versus "diversity." In other words, it is not enough for school personnel to state that "we accept diversity." Multiculturalism must move beyond once-a-year celebrations of diversity, "international foods night," or a chapter on Asian American history. Rather, difference must be thought of both at the level of the subject/individual and at the group level through race, class, sex, age, and so forth, whereby structures of identity and power are historically connected and interrogated. Such an approach does not have to essentialize difference, but should approach power as relative. One approach toward demonstrating the relativity of power is by encouraging students to see difference through similarity. This can be done through the following examinations: (1) the cultural differences and similarities of student investments in cultural forms, such as rock music; (2) struggles over identity and representation within television and cinema, moving beyond the analysis of the media's hegemonic influences; (3) disapora and home/homelessness—how "minority" or "marginalized" students create and find homes within and outside the dominant structures, becoming "border crossers" (Giroux, 1992); and (4) deconstructing whiteness—taking apart a multiculturalism rooted in a "democratic imaginary" (Laclau & Mouffe, 1985).

In accordance with critical postmodernism and multiculturalism, the goals of critical pedagogy should transgress progressive pedagogical approaches. As Lawrence Grossberg describes in his introduction to *Between Borders* (1994), there are three philosophical models of a progressive pedagogy, all of which deserve critique. First, there is the hierarchical model, in which the teacher's goal is to teach "truths" to students. This is the model that most critical pedagogues have critiqued (Freire, Giroux, Shor, etc.). Second, the dialogical model of pedagogy aims to encourage silenced students to speak (see Shor, 1992). For example, Shor situates critical pedagogy through personal empowerment whereby the goal of education is geared toward the self and social change as "the self and society create each other" through voice and dialogue. Unfortunately, the problem with this model is that it assumes students aren't already speaking in ways teachers can understand or demand, or that there aren't serious material and social conditions that disenable students from speaking at particular moments in particular forms. Third, the praxical pedagogy is one (previously defined through the theorists above—namely McLaren, Giroux, Shor) in which students are to intervene in their own history and fight for public spaces that encourage democratic participation. The problem with this model is that it assumes that students aren't already invested in transforming their own history and that the teacher has the right knowledge and skills through which to make such transformations and emancipation possible. Consequently, given these critiques, a new model of critical pedagogy should be conceptualized.

It is through Grossberg's pedagogy of risk and articulation that the goals of critical pedagogy should be retheorized philosophically and pragmatically. First, a pedagogy of risk and articulation begins by arguing that teachers must go beyond traditional notions of intellectual authority without dismissing claims to authority. Additionally, the teacher needs to acknowledge her/his role within the institutionalized power structure of schools as well. Teachers should not assume to know in advance the necessary knowledge, language, and skills of students; rather, through the contextual, teachers should take risks by interrogating forms, drawing lines, mapping articulations between discourses, domains, and practices. Accordingly, theory and politics, or theoretical and political correctness, cannot be determined in advance (Grossberg).

Moreover, within a pedagogy of articulation and risk, the goals and outcomes of the learning process cannot be known in advance. In other words, students should be encouraged to determine for themselves their futures in unimagined and unimaginable ways. This may mean going beyond illusory goals or notions such as "democracy" and "emancipation." Chantal Mouffe (1993) realizes that common interests, consensus, and unanimity are illusory goals. For her, "a healthy democratic process calls for a vibrant clash of political positions and an open conflict of interests" (cited in Robins, 1996, p. 24). It might make more sense, then, to reconfigure altruistic goals like democracy through "a political framework that can accommodate difference and antagonism to sustain what Mouffe calls an 'agonistic pluralism' " (Robins, 1996, p. 24). Through this paradigmatic pedagogical shift, students need to define for themselves "the political" through the intersections of their locations, experiences, and concrete practices with historical and/or social representations of experience (Mohanty, 1994, p. 154). Hence the goal of teachers (and critical pedagogy) should not be to move students from one location or position to another, encouraging them to submit to or accept the political notions, ethics, and ideals espoused by the "radical" teacher. Rather, the goals of critical pedagogy should be to encourage students to identify their practices and complicitness in the political, popular, and cultural realm, allowing them to create new possibilities and new organizational spaces for their future. This approach can be associated with Masterman's notion of critical autonomy.

While Ira Shor's notions of *Empowering Education* (1992) advance a dialogical pedagogical model preoccupied with modernist ideals of "democracy" and "empowerment," his model of "problem-posing" versus "problem-solving" is extremely useful in applying the goals of critical pedagogy within a model of risk and articulation. Rather than privilege simple solutions to complex problems by asking students to spit out "the correct answer" as determined by the teacher, problem-posing allows students use their experiences and diverse perspectives to address those social issues that concern them and their communities. This allows for new organizations of spaces to emerge as students travel and explore new possibilities and ways of understanding society, culture, identity, and knowledge. By connecting problem-posing with media literacy theory and production, students can best address the issues that directly affect their lives and futures. We will return to problem-posing when we critically engage with information in cyberspace, as it requires comparing and contrasting mediated "reality" with personal and experiential-based reality.

## CRITICAL CULTURAL STUDIES AND POPULAR CULTURE

In this final section, we will examine the central theoretical tenets of critical cultural studies and the study of popular culture in order to examine how the use of new telecommunications technology in schools perpetuates a hegemonic force in which the business community defines the curricular uses of computer skills rather than educators committed to a liberal arts education. Just as Stan Denski and David Sholle (1994) argue that the use of video equipment in most liberal arts programs creates a hegemonic influence that normalizes the dominant production methods and predefines career needs, we will see how the current use of computer/online technology in schools perpetuates or reproduces a similar cultural hegemony. Furthermore, the theories articulated here will make it possible for us to look at how information available on the Internet is affected by graphic design elements and advertising that naturalize and predetermine the possibilities of Web-page design and our understanding of how information can be sought, organized, and retrieved through a decentralized form of technology. As with all communications technology, capitalist interests have defined the content and structure of the media soon after its inception. But since there is no intrinsic formula defining the content and structure of the Internet, it is vital that classroom curriculum and pedagogy take learning in a new direction by teaching students to venture into otherwise unknown enclaves located within this predominantly commercial terrain. Students need to differentiate between various sources of information using critical thinking skills and an understanding of political economy in order to keep in play the contest and struggle over meaning. This is not to suggest that students are uncritical thinkers or that the Internet as a medium is completely invested with the politics of commodification. Rather, through a pedagogy of risk and experimentation, our goal will be to articulate how teachers *and* students can together inform what questions and investigations need to become part of critical learning, and what actions need to be taken upon such exploration.

Although cultural studies is a disciplinary field without a uniform definition, methodology, approach, or practice (Stuart Hall [1992] claims cultural studies is not just one thing), I will attempt to discuss some of the important and relevant themes within the field as they have been conceptualized by the Birmingham School of British Cultural Studies. Within the study of mass communication comes a long history of various approaches to media or popular cultural forms that asks interesting but impractical questions about the "effects" of the media on our views and perceptions of the "culture" or the world. Unlike most traditional approaches to the analysis of the media (effects research, uses and gratifications, textual analysis, etc.), research stemming from Dr. George Gerbner's cultural indicators project (1978) poses and addresses three important core questions, namely:

1. *Who gets to tell the stories of our culture?* This allows for the study of the institutional analysis of the media or popular forms or the political economy of the media.
2. *What is the content of these stories?* (textual analysis).
3. *How do these stories impact audiences?* (audience analysis).

Through an analysis of Antonio Gramsci's notion of hegemony (1971) and Louis Althusser's conception of ideological state apparatuses (1971), cultural studies goes beyond an orthodox Marxist approach by expanding Marx's conception of capital as the ultimate determinational force of culture.[7] It seeks to examine the many "cultures" that exist within society and within various groups and variables (e.g., race, class, gender, etc). But although cultural studies goes beyond the notion of capital as the ultimate determination of ideology, it nevertheless retains a vested interest in examining the institutional forces that limit and "encode" our culture through capital and ruling ideologies. This area of cultural studies examines how the conglomeration of media through mergers and monopolies serves to delimit a plurality of voices and/or cultural forms and expressions. Cultural studies is concerned with issues of power and struggles over meaning within media, history, culture, art, and so forth.

Without imposing a high culture/low culture distinction, cultural studies treats all cultural forms as "texts," so that the production of meanings is studied and examined within and among all cultural forms of expression. Whereas other approaches toward the study of culture have downplayed the importance of popular forms, cultural studies understands culture as those aspects that are part of everyday life; as Paul Willis (1977) describes, culture refers to our everyday practices— "the bricks and mortar of our most commonplace understandings" (cited in Grossberg, Nelson, & Triechler, 1992, p. 4). By defining culture through everyday life, cultural studies allows us to examine the production of meaning as articulated within particular contexts and practices. Through "deconstruction," textual analysis allows us to take apart those taken-for-granted "stories" or narratives that give us our commonsense knowledges of how the world works and what our roles within it are. Through poststructuralism, cultural studies allows us to debunk the "canons" that have traditionally accorded ruling-class ideologies and aesthetics a privileged place within culture. Questions of identity—how it is produced, "articulated, experienced and deployed" (p. 9)—remain central within cultural studies, as evidenced in studies on race, ethnicity, and postcolonialism. Likewise, feminism has informed cultural studies by raising questions about subjectivity, gender, politics, and desire.

Cultural studies as an approach recognizes that the hegemonic or ideological forces that aim to foreclose meaning and understanding are not without their limits. Culture is transacted between consumers and producers, not simply laid on people from above (Agger, 1992). However, the more Marxist the approach, "the less emphasis is placed on the active role of consumers in determining cultural meaning" (p. 8). Accordingly, cultural studies examines how audiences are active rather than passive agents who can challenge and resist mediated messages about culture. Despite their political and/or economic ties, the media (or the "culture industry," as Theodor Adorno and Max Horkheimer [1972] would conceive them) do not impose their "values" or ideological positions onto "dupes" who are unresponsive or uncritical consumers. Consequently, in understanding how popular meanings are produced, cultural studies moves beyond a theory of hegemony through Hall's theory of articulation, which allows us to examine "the continual severing, realigning, and recombining of discourses, social groups, political interests, and structures of power within society" (Grossberg, Nelson, & Triechler, 1992, p. 8). Hence "the meaning of popular cultural forms can only be ascertained through their articulation" within a set of practices or as "historically specific contextual relations" that determine political meaning and ideological interests (Giroux and Simon, 1989, p. 9). As Hall reminds us, what is important is not the intrinsic or historically fixed object(s) of culture, but the state of play within cultural relations (in Grossberg, Nelson, & Triechler, 1992).

Although Hall, Laclau, and Mouffe's theory of articulation moves beyond Gramsci's notion of hegemony, we need to address the importance of hegemony as a concept in the study of popular culture, pedagogy, and media literacy. First, unlike theories of "domination" or "power" that understand the imposition of ideology or power through overt force and/or punishment, hegemony works within the terrain of everyday life and requires the consent of audiences/citizens/the masses. Hegemony raises a number of theoretical questions about how power, as a cultural, economic, political, and pedagogical force, aims to define, organize, and legitimate particular conceptions of common sense. In Gramsci's view, the process of reaching consent through common sense is achieved through the continual (inter)play between the cultural and ideological domain of subordinate groups in order to sanction the interests and authority of the ruling block (Giroux and Simon, 1989, p. 8). Yet unlike Adorno and Horkheimer's analysis of the culture industry (1972), in which capital prevails as the dominant ideological force, hegemony allows us to study how power is continually struggled for/over.

As in critical cultural studies, the dual concepts of hegemony and ideology function concurrently to substantiate the need for critical pedagogy. According to critical pedagogues Giroux and Simon (1989), Gramsci's concept of hegemony is both a political and a pedagogical process:

> Moral leadership and state power are tied to a process of consent, as a form of practical learning, which is secured through the elaboration of particular discourses, needs, appeals, values, and interests that must address and transform the concerns of subordinate groups. In this perspective, hegemony is a continuing, shifting, and problematic historical process. Consent is structured through a series of relations marked by an ongoing political struggle over competing conceptions and views of the world between dominant and subcultural groups. (p. 8)

It is through this struggle for consent that the task of critical pedagogy merges with cultural studies in its objective to

> unmask hegemonies and critique ideologies with the political and ethical intent of helping to empower students and, more generally, the social groups to which they belong: by fostering awareness of

conditions that limit possibilities for human becoming and legitimate the unequal distribution of social goods (Gee 1991); and by unveiling the origins and the historical contingency of these ideologies/hegemonies and the social relations and practices they simultaneously beget and sustain. (Lankshear, Peters, & Knobel, 1996, p. 150–51)

Hence the struggle for power is never about "pure victory or pure domination . . . it is never a zero-sum cultural game" (Hall, 1993, p. 24). It is always a struggle over the balance of power within/between cultural relations. Thus, in accordance with analyses of hegemony as a political and pedagogical process, we will also look at "alternative" Web sites in the subsequent chapters, in order to observe the state of interplay between cultural forces.

## NOTES

1. By "media savvy," I am referring to the general experiences we incur through everyday interactions and encounters with media in a variety of forms.

2. My continual reference to the terms *critical thinking, critical consumption*, and *critical citizenry* are not meant to privilege an interpretive paradigm that "reveals" the true or correct ideological meanings and messages of texts. As Ava Collins (1994) explains, the privileging of such paradigms carries with it the same consequences for the left as it does for the right. As I will explain through a theory of risk and articulation, I do not purpose critical thinking as a means to the acquisition of intrinsic knowledge espoused by the radical teacher who is always necessarily wiser than her/his students. Instead, I believe that critical thinking must be conceptualized as a discourse, a joint venture between informed and experienced students *and* teachers engaged in defining knowledge for themselves in particular contexts. This does not mean that the teacher loses claims to knowledge or authority, but that her/his pedagogy must be reconceptualized.

3. Although I am using the term *democracy*, I am not using it in the traditional (idealistic) sense of the definition as a consensus-forming practice reflecting ideals of "the people," but rather as a principle espousing social equality/ respect for all individuals within a community.

4. The eight key media literacy concepts examined here are adapted from the *Media Literacy Resource Guide* (1989) published by the Ontario Ministry of Education and were rearticulated during the 1993 Media Literacy National Leadership Conference on Media Literacy, held in Aspen, Colorado. These principles are the underlying foundation of many media literacy training workshops as well as introductory reading material.

5. As described by Michael Morgan and Nancy Signorielli (1990), cultivation analysis represents a particular set of theoretical and methodological assumptions and procedures designed to assess the contributions of television viewing to people's conceptions of social reality.

6. Here Masterman is referring to John Dewey's optimism and emphasis upon education as both schooling and, more important, a mode of democratic politics (*Democracy and Education*, 1916). Dewey's notion of democracy emerged from his pragmatic philosophy and theory of progressive education.

7. Gramsci's concept of hegemony clarifies how cultural power is able to penetrate into the terrain of daily life, which is a site of struggle and consent. Likewise, Althusser suggests that ideology is "lived practice," not simply imposed from the outside.

# 4

## Easy Solutions for Complex Problems: Internet Restrictions and Resources

With the growth and popularity of the Internet within the last few years has come a whole host of issues, such as the growing presence of children and minors on the Internet. One of the major contentions concerns inappropriate content. Fears over students stumbling across indecent text, images, and video, both legal and illegal, either in the form of e-mail or on the Net, include concerns about exposure to pornography, racism, sexism, abusive language, and solicitation. The groundbreaking case that incited much controversy occurred early in 1995. Featured on the broadcast news entertainment program *Inside Edition*, a suspected pedophile was caught soliciting a fourteen-year-old child in an online chat room. What the suspect did not know was that the fourteen-year-old was actually an undercover police officer in the state of Florida. Another incident of online abuse that received national attention occurred in 1995 at the University of Michigan. Then undergraduate Jake Baker e-mailed and posted violent sexual fantasies to a Usenet group; in one of them, the name of the victim was a female classmate. The university promptly suspended Baker, and he was charged with interstate transmission of a threat, a federal crime. At Boston College, racist hate mail was sent to thirteen minority students using e-mail, likening them to animals and suggesting they leave a college the writer described as "for white men" (Flaherty, 1998). Boston College is one of several colleges and universities to see hateful e-mail sent on their systems, including the University of Nebraska at Lincoln and the University of North Carolina.

Naturally, most K–12 schools, colleges, and universities are concerned about the material being sent and acquired from their servers and have devised "quasi-solutions" to deal with these issues. This chapter will examine the measures proposed to assist parents, legislators, educators, and the public within an educational context that values critical learning and autonomy over commercial regulation. By addressing the advantages and shortcomings of these initiatives, we will be advancing a critical, information literacy approach directed at student learning, which will lead us to the consecutive chapter. Although we will not be personally testing and rating the function and utility of the software products mentioned, we will be analyzing the marketing strategies used to sell these products and will survey the objectives and limits of such products. Among the following solutions mentioned are those adapted from the Internet Parental Control (IPC) Frequently Asked Questions (provided by the Voters Telecommunications Watch), the Platform for Internet Content Selection (PICS), the Recreational Software Advisory Council on the Internet (RSACi), and CyberPatrol, Cybersitter, Net Nanny, SafeSurf, and SurfWatch.

## INOCULATION, REGULATION, OR MEDIA LITERACY? CURRENT RESPONSES TO INTERNET CONTENT

Though a wide range of measures are currently being proposed to deal with inappropriate content, parental guidance is usually the first solution advanced as the most effective method of getting comfortable with a child's access to the Internet. The underlying premise for this choice of solution is that no other person except the parent knows best what is or isn't appropriate for their child. As the IPC maintains, by learning to use the Internet with the child, the parent can instill in their child the values they want them to use when selecting material on the Internet, as on television, radio, or in print media: "The respect built between you and your child will function when no one is around, and will survive software upgrades, eternally-changing international law, and other unpredictable events" (Safdar & Cherry, 1995–1996). According to the IPC, this solution is supported as the best one by most reasonable parents and free speech advocates.

It's not surprising that such a solution is touted as "the best" by members of the IPC. After all, they are a group of parents organized to disseminate "solutions" for those concerned about the information electronically available to their children. Nevertheless, despite the numerous problems with this proposition, my main objection is that it espouses an individualized, rather than organizational or systemic, mobilization. Although the IPC does not believe in government censorship, it nevertheless offers an approach that essentially allows parents the power to withhold material from their children. Aside from the major political ramifications embroiled within this logic, the IPC's approach also reifies altruistic assumptions about parent/child relations. Not only would most children, teens, and young adults be much more antagonistic about this level of control or "guidance," but most parents would be hard-pressed for the time involved in this hand-holding approach.

On the other hand, governmental restrictions pose another set of difficulties. As explained by the IPC, some members of Congress have introduced legislation to criminalize certain types of speech throughout the medium in order to safeguard minors from objectionable material. But as they point out, although this plays well at the polls, it is not effective at addressing the issue of children's access to such material: "As long as the Internet continues to be a global network, there will always be some one or more countries in which one can provide material that is out of the reach of US law and flies afoul of US expression standards" (Safdar & Cherry, 1995–1996). What's more, constitutional restrictions on speech are extremely difficult to produce. While we need not be totally opposed to government regulation, especially in the area of advertising, this issue begs the question: What are the grounds for censure? This leads to a complicated scenario where various political, religious, commercial, and parental groups lobby for the regulation of material that threatens their own aims.[1]

Proof-of-age/shielding systems are yet another form of content filtering. Essentially, these systems require that a user be over age eighteen to access a particular site, which fact is verified through credit card. Yet it is not too hard to envision a child or young adult tampering with this system by simply obtaining a parent's credit card number. Although this may be a legitimate and reasonable method through which to redirect youth and children from unsuitable Web sites, the larger problem is that this option does not address the importance of teaching students critical discernment.[2] Ironically, the IPC is more concerned about the "moral hazard" of a reduced advertising audience size resulting from the screening out of minors. For them, third-party approaches are better at aligning the incentives of all participants. The limit of this counterattack is that it doesn't consider the problems with electronic advertising directed at children or youth. Within the IPC "parental guidance" measure, advertising is not considered to be a major contributor to "the instillation of values." We will return to this serious omission later.

In accordance with shielding or blocking systems, there are several online systems that have proprietary environments available, where content is screened as being available for the lowest common denominator of children (Safdar & Cherry, 1995–1996). The parent requests that the child's account be placed into this environment. America On-line (AOL) provides parental blocking that allows either limitation of a child's selected screen-name to either a "Kids Only" area, which is recommended for children under twelve, or restriction on the use of chat rooms or newsgroups by preteens and teens (Safdar & Cherry, 1995–1996). According to the IPC, "Kids Only" is a collection of edu-cational resources and entertainment areas as well as a preselected collection of child-oriented Internet sites, with AOL staff monitoring of message boards and chat rooms. There's also an AOL parental phone line for parents to find instructions and advice on choosing and main-taining the settings of this product. Despite the IPC's assurance that this "customer-driven feature" increases the reliability of the service, it nevertheless remains dependent upon a commercial Internet service provider.

## DEALING WITH "INAPPROPRIATE" CONTENT IN SCHOOLS

Within an educational setting, there are additional measures that can be taken by teachers and administrators to fend off the electronic inflow of inappropriate information or visuals. One tentative solution devised by most elementary, secondary, and postsecondary educational institutions is a student usage agreement designed to encourage spe-cific codes of conduct to be followed in the new medium. This allows schools to discipline students who abuse Internet access by plagiarizing through the use of research-paper mills, cyber-stalking others, or send-ing hate mail. Most schools have usage "contracts" to keep students responsible for their actions rather than giving responsibility to ad-ministrators or educators. One example from a middle school details a student code of conduct (outlined below) that students must agree to and sign prior to receiving a login ID and password to use the school's computer systems. It stipulates the following rules:

- Obey any local, state, or federal laws or rules on technology or copyright licensing.
- Treat all computer equipment with the utmost care and respect and not willfully cause damage to said equipment.
- Not do anything that might jeopardize the integrity of the school's network.
- Use only your own login and password and not share them with anyone.

- Not use another student's or teacher's password, programs, or files.
- Use only those applications or files assigned by a teacher.
- Not trespass into menus, applications, or files not given specific access to, such as system administration, teacher, or school accounts.
- Not use/load/run disks that are not from the school, including all personal disks, programs, or files from home or other nonschool agencies, therefore eliminating the potential of infecting the school system with a virus.
- Not waste electronic storage space by saving unnecessary or frivolous files or programs.
- Not use the network or Internet for commercial, obscene, or illegal purposes.
- Respect commonly accepted practices on Internet etiquette.
- Not use inappropriate, offensive, foul, or abusive language.
- Not send or display obscene or offensive messages or pictures.
- Not harass by sending annoying, obscene, libelous, threatening, or anonymous messages.
- Not respond or reply to inappropriate messages.
- Respect other users' rights to privacy.
- Navigate the Internet and use any information at your own risk.

In addition to an explanation of the penalties for any violation of the above, such conduct codes usually include disclaimers, making students aware that although the Internet may provide an array of educational information from a variety of sources, some of the accessed materials may be obscene, abusive, offensive, defamatory, inaccurate, or illegal. This serves as a safeguard for schools and teachers so that they are not held accountable in the event that such material is accessed. At the K–12 level, it is not unusual for parents to be asked to sign the policy in addition to the student.

While usage agreements are fairly standard, some schools have responded to concerns about Internet exploitation and inappropriate content by aiming for tighter control. One approach is to filter information by adopting Internet rating systems. Much like the rating system for television content, Internet rating systems, as well as filtering techniques based on electronic labels, have been devised to encourage users to be warned of inappropriate, indecent, or obscene content. Some of these systems include the aforementioned PICS and RSACi, as well as the Internet Voluntary Self-Rating (IVSR), which relies totally on self-rating by site creators.

Designed by the Massachusetts Institute of Technology's World Wide Web Consortium, PICS enables people to create and distribute labels that describe Web sites in a coherent and easily readable way. Although PICS is not a rating system or software program, it provides a set of technical protocols that enable software and rating services to process these labels so that users are shielded from unwanted information or directed to potentially useful sites. According to Paul Resnick (1997), chair of the PICS working group of the World Wide Web Consortium, PICS was originally designed to allow parents and teachers to review questionable materials that they wouldn't want children to come across on the Net. Unlike government legislation, such as the Communications Decency Act, PICS allows Internet users to regulate incoming information. By describing any part of a Web site or document, Resnick explains that the first labels check for items that might not be in accordance with local indecency laws.

Another program, RSACi, applied its criteria for rating computer games to the Internet using four rating scores on each label to denote the levels of violence, nudity, sex, and potentially offensive language (Resnick, 1997). RSACi also enables a Web author to self-rate her or his site by filling out a questionnaire (at www.rsac.org), after which RSACi sends back a set of hypertext markup language (HTML) tags that authors can include in their pages (Safdar & Cherry, 1995–1996). The IVSR program, created by Alex Stewart, similarly enables Web-site labeling (www.crl.com/~riche/ivsr/proposal.html).

In theory, these rating systems present some benefits in steering kids and youth away from some areas that might be deemed offensive. However, on a practical level, the systems are not uniform and are sometimes confusing to Internet users. One site might self-rate using very different criteria than would another, similar site. Moreover, there is no guarantee that the authors of Web sites would willingly comply in a self-rating system.

Consequently, some schools have opted to go one step further through the purchase and installation of restrictive software programs, such as Net Nanny or Internet Filter. Net Nanny (www.netnanny.com) is a tool allowing parents, teachers, or administrators to screen information acquired from, as well as sent to, the Internet. It can also prevent children from accessing files on a PC's hard drive, floppy, or CD-ROM. Like audit tracking software, Net Nanny keeps a record of a child's or student's Internet perusal. Likewise, Internet Filter (www.internetfilter.com) is a control tool for Microsoft Windows (version 95) that can be configured to block or log all data transfers, including World Wide Web pages, newsgroups, types of messages within any newsgroup, Internet Relay

Chat, or Internet hosts known to have material objectionable for children (Safdar & Cherry, 1995–1996). Both programs are available for approximately $50.

Third-party rating systems, such as SurfWatch, Cybersitter, and CyberPatrol, offer restrictive control tools for material they've found objectionable. These systems do more than label Web sites; they prevent access to questionable material using blocking devices based on specific sites, or based on key words and phrases. Moreover, they allow parents, teachers, and administrators to set up trigger phrases and words ahead of time. If these phrases or words are detected in the "data stream," the software will either shut down the computer, block the transmission, or disconnect the modem. Each system operates differently. Offered by Microsystems Software for roughly $50, CyberPatrol (www.cyberpatrol.com) allows parents to control or limit access to certain times of day, or to control or limit the total amount of usage per day or week. Through the use of its objectionable sites list, CyberPatrol can also block access to specific Web sites, or can block sites specified by the program user.

Although it is designed for parental supervision, SurfWatch (www.surfwatch.com) is a similar program that prevents access to Web, gopher, and ftp sites that SurfWatch's team of "Net-surfers" have found objectionable. The site maintains an updated list of "not-for-children" Web sites that can be subscribed to electronically. Cybersitter (cybersitter.com) works by filtering predefined offensive sites, newsgroups, chat rooms, and the like, a list of which are held in an updated filter file. Offered by Solid Oak Software, Inc., for $29.95, this program has "smart phrase technology" to predict and alert parents and teachers to other potentially offensive sites and can block offensive words and language in incoming and outgoing e-mail. It can also track the Internet sites that have been visited, for later review by parents or teachers.

Although serious discussion about government regulation goes beyond the purview of this study, several concerns must be raised regarding these commercial software programs. First, as previously mentioned, the decision to block some sites over others is a very subjective decision. The problem with this kind of regulation is that some groups and individuals might attempt to censor (under the guise of concerns for "safety") material that threatens their own political and/or religious agendas. Second, some of the trigger words used to block Internet sites might be legitimate subjects for research. For example, a user wouldn't be able to access research on breast cancer or sex education if the words *breast* and *sex* were denoted as trigger words. Third, students and computer hackers have already found flaws within such programs and have managed to acquire information from sites that have been blocked. And finally, information filtering doesn't prepare us to learn how to analyze and evaluate information once we are no longer using the Internet within an educational setting.

The final method of dealing with inappropriate Internet material is to establish adult monitoring in schools through both on-site adult monitors who maintain a watchful presence over student Internet usage, and audit tracking software that records the sites frequented by students. Unfortunately, most schools are short on the kind of staffing needed to provide "in-person" monitoring. Moreover, the amount of time needed to check the sites attended by students, as tracked within the audit logs, poses another inconvenience.

## MARKETING ON "CYBER SAFE-SITES"

Although some of these Internet resources and restrictions make sense for certain schools depending upon the age group and grade level of Internet users, we have observed some of the problematic areas within each method. The underlying difficulty raised by these "quasi-solutions" is that they narrowly define what is "inappropriate," relegating most objections to issues of nudity, sexuality, trigger words, or adult content. This neglects to confront the invasion of advertising or marketing strategies directed at children. In many respects, this seems to be a more serious concern. First, although child-directed advertising might not be as blatantly offensive, it certainly fosters "values," which is the underlying concern specified by the IPC group. The first tenet of media literacy outlined in the previous chapter explains that *all media are constructions*. The problem with advertising is that it is so much a part of our social landscape, our everyday life, that it appears to be natural. Subsequently, the conceptualization of what is inappropriate for children or students is confined to sustain the interests of a commercial system through the omission of advertising. Just as concerned scholars, teachers, and parents have raised eyebrows when realizing the profit-making agenda—advertising to students—of cable programs broadcast in schools like Channel One, we need to be equally circumspect about the amount of advertising and marketing designated to "Kids Only" sites.

Moreover, the proposals outlined above sustain a cyber-market economy in which consumer software programs become the antidote to inappropriate material rather than public discourse, political action, or critical media literacy skills. The products previously analyzed are produced and distributed by profit-making computer companies, such as computer giant Microsoft, Sun Systems, Solid Oak, and the like. Obviously, for profit-making companies, it is good business to create and sell blocking software products or to offer third-party rating systems that decide for parents or educators what's in their (both children's and the company's) best interest. In a self-fulfilling business transaction, reports of inappropriate content and media hype about the Internet as an "unsafe environment" lend credence to, or create a functionalist need for, such products. As stated earlier, advertising is overlooked as "inappropriate content," in part because it is part of the everyday—unlike pornography, nudity, or obscenities, which are probably not as common, at least for children. As Antonio Gramsci (1971) noted, hegemony works within the terrain of everyday life and requires the consent of audiences—or in this case, parents and educators. I would argue that the rhetorical elements creating cyber-paranoia within the mainstream attempt to reach the consent of parents and educators by inviting them to see some Internet content as value-laden or problematic—cyberporn, obscenities, and the like—while camouflaging the interests and authority of profitable computer software and hardware industries, blinding them from seeing advertising to children and young adults as a serious issue.

This hegemonic impulse becomes clear when we take a look at some Web sites recommended or selected by third-party rating systems as well as by software filtering products. Let's begin with SafeSurf (www.safesurf.com), a rating organization that claims to be "dedicated to making the Internet safe for your children without censorship." According to this rating system, "there is more to be gained than just the free flow of information." Through an information classification system, SafeSurf believes they "will enable software and hardware to be developed that will enable more effective use of the Internet for *everyone*" (emphasis added).

My skepticism about claims that "everyone" benefits through a "classification system" developed when visiting the SafeSurf home page. What first drew my attention on the home page had nothing to do with the services offered, but pertained to the advertisements centered on the page. One ad displayed a large, colorful rectangular for Card Service Online, "the leader in online real time credit card processing," featuring MasterCard, VISA, Discover, and American Express. Directly under it was an ad for *Child Magazine*, on sale at the reduced price of $7.95, its pitch: "One year for the price of a bottle." Beneath this was a bold advertisement link to "Update Microsoft's Internet Explorer to support SafeSurf Ratings." Combined, these ads validated my forewarning about the interconnections between big profit-making computer firms, such as Microsoft, and software blocking products.

My findings led me to presume that more advertising would emerge on the SafeSurf "Wave" link, which offers "Kid's Wave," a list of "top sites" purportedly "devoted to educating and entertaining children." On the "Kid's Wave" home page, I was informed: "There are great places to take your children online." Below was a grid of partial listings of

SafeSurf-approved sites by category. The first category was the "favorite site of the month," which was "Squigly's Playhouse." By clicking on the cartoon graphic, my hypothesis was reaffirmed: the unfolding visual displayed a large color advertisement for Disneyland with moving graphics and a photo of the Magic Kingdom. The flashing text read: (frame 1—photo and text depicted Disneyland Resort) "To really enjoy yourself here" (frame 2—photo of Mickey Mouse described as "the Disneyland Trip Wizard") "Pick up your custom schedule here."

In case the ad was overlooked, each separate, clickable "Kid's Wave" link for an activity or game was infused with ads. For instance, the "Squigly's Games" page had another large, flashing, color ad for Disney at the top that read: (frame 1—photo of Mickey Mouse) "Are you the Ultimate Disney fan?"; (frame 2—photo of Goofy) "Click here—enter to win." On the bottom, a three-frame flashing ad targeted at parents read: (frame 1) "You know what you put on your card"; (frame 2) "but do you know what *he* put on your card?" (picture of a crowd with a man circled in red); (frame 3) "Find out with your free credit report online." Other pages, like "Squigly's Writing Corner" or "Brainteasers," had separate Disney ads as well as credit card ads (presumably targeted at parents, but also at a new generation of consumers).

While not all rating systems carried advertising to the same extreme, similar findings were made on Internet sites for filtering software products. In addition to selling nonsoftware products, such as $40 embroidered golf shirts, Net Nanny's Web site had an advertisement for Disneyland featured on its front page. Among its "safe-sites" for kids were "fun" links to Disney, Crayola, and Kids Channel. Under the category "Education" was a Colgate "Kidsworld" link with prominent product advertisements for Colgate toothpaste. Describing its mission in philanthropic terms, Colgate Palmolive purportedly maintains the Internet site "as a service to the Internet community." A closer look at the page proves otherwise. First, I had to type in my first name and specified password of the day, "toothpaste," in order to enter the "No Cavities Clubhouse." There, I was greeted by "Dr. Rabbit," who appeared in his clubhouse holding a toothbrush and Colgate toothpaste. Although this Web site offered "interesting oral care facts, games, and stories aimed at raising children's awareness of oral health," I couldn't get away from "Dr. Rabbit" and his Colgate endorsement no matter what activity I clicked on. Moreover, in spite of Net Nanny's "intention" to adhere to the Children's Advertising Review Unit (CARU) guidelines for advertising on the Internet and online services, my name and e-mail address were still requested so that the "Tooth Fairy" could send me an e-mail message—no doubt carrying her Colgate toothpaste and brush in cyber-flight.

Although not nearly as plastered in advertising as SafeSurf or Net

Nanny, CyberPatrol's Web site did allow for the acquisition of commercial Web sites. Upon navigating the special kids' section, "Route 6-16 Cyber Guide," I was asked to type into a search engine a category that I might find of interest. I typed in "games," and among the many offered to me were various computer games for sale, like Mindscape, which when clicked brought me to the Mindscape home page. For instance, the Mindscape site advertised its game Imperialism II (for $49) through graphics, description, and simulation.

Another recommended "safe-site" was *Toy Story* Games, a game developed by Disney based on its *Toy Story* movie. Not surprisingly, Disney's home page was chock-full of child- and adult-directed advertising.[3] Although the advertising contained here was "2nd level," meaning that I had to click on the recommended sites before being inundated with ads, the sites contained on the page remained uncontested as child-appropriate.

As evidenced within these "kid"-designated Web sites, the far-reaching clutches of advertisers are rendered invisible in the discourse or underlying rationale of Internet protectionism. While children are deemed to be impressionable when it comes to sex, pornography, adult content, and nefarious language, concerns about manipulative advertising campaigns go largely undetected within "cyber-safe" domains. As stated earlier, this perpetuates the hegemonic force of already powerful computer software and hardware enterprises.

Not only is there "manufactured consent" among software rating and blocking companies regarding the benignity of advertising, but the special interests of those underwriting the Internet policies previously examined are unmistakable when we look at the emerging partnerships between computer corporations and Internet rating systems. On February 28, 1996, corporate mammoth Microsoft announced it was joining efforts with RSACi "to advance parental control over Internet access and content" (www.bilkent.edu.tr/pub/www/pics/960228/microsoft. html). By offering a new rating system combining RSACi and Microsoft's "Content Advisory" feature, parents would be allowed to monitor and screen the content viewed by their children through a new version of Microsoft's Internet Explorer Web browser.

Microsoft is not alone in its desire to ensure a partnership with RSACi, but is paralleled by other software vendors like Microsystems Software and SurfWatch Software, which are adapting their products to be compatible with the PICS specifications and RSACi solutions. One week after Microsoft announced its partnership with RSACi, AT&T sent out a press release announcing its selection of the Microsystems Internet filtering tool, CyberPatrol, for its World Network Service (www.bilkent.edu.tr / pub / WWW / PICS / 960306? ATT-andMicro Systems.html).[4] Together the two companies decided to produce and offer their own "solution" to parental controls. Through a marketing approach that designates responsibility for content selection to the individual, AT&T offers its WorldNet customers a thirty-day demo version of CyberPatrol, after which it can be purchased for about $30. This includes a three month subscription to the "CyberNOT Block" list, which contains over 7,000 researched Internet sites that might have questionable material. Unfortunately, as with most of these products, the determining criteria for the block list are not explicated in detail, although we do know that they are broadly based on "violence, sexual themes, nudity, or potentially offensive language" (Lewis, 1996).

In a cross-lateral integrative move, Microsoft has offered to make its "Content Advisor" software freely available to other companies to use in the creation of compatible rating systems and browsers. Naturally, this will lead to "more of the same" in terms of the representativeness of rating systems and products, and will allow Microsoft to continue to set the terms of (and eventually dominate) software products. Yet in order to assist RSACi in their rating standards, there has been much cooperation and vertical integration of software, hardware, and technical resources from Microsoft and other industry partners to power the RSACi Web site (www.bilkent.edu.tr/pub/WWW/PICS/960228/Microsoft.html). According to the press release from Microsoft, the RSACi Web site will be powered through two dual-Pentium Dell PowerEdge servers running the Microsoft BackOffice family and the Microsoft Internet Information Server (IIS). While the article didn't explain the function and utility of these impressive systems, it's quite clear that the level of investments and cooperative initiatives by computer firms aren't purely philanthropic. As Peter Lewis (1996) explains, although ratings are voluntarily assigned by the producers of software, most software publishers are participating in or supporting the system because many retailers decline to sell software without ratings. For instance, retailers like Wal-Mart have used the RSACi system to help them select what software products to sell in their stores (Lewis, 1996). Thus, without a rating, software companies stand a chance of losing access to retailers and, in turn, foregoing profits.

Aside from the free advertising of products registered by Microsoft, Intel, and Dell, the "donations" made to run the RSACi Web site are said to help "empower the public"; yet no public forum displaying alternative methods, solutions, or measures has been considered. In fact, just as private health insurance companies were eager to overthrow a single-payer health care system subsidized by the government a few years ago in spite of populist support, software companies have likewise staked their territory by continually denouncing government regulation of cyberspace. According to Lewis, announcements by Microsoft, SurfWatch, and CyberPatrol to back rating systems for the Internet

constitute "the strongest response yet by the Internet software community to recent attempts by federal and state legislators to protect
children by regulating the content of the Internet and on-line services."
This explains why Microsoft, along with thirty businesses and organizations, "joined in lawsuits challenging the constitutionality of the
Communications Decency Act, which places control of Internet content
in the hands of the federal government" (Lewis, 1996). Hence it stands
to reason that RSACi's rating system emerged from a group of mainly
private companies/organizations, including the World Wide Web Consortium, AT&T Bell Laboratories, Bell Atlantic, and Mediascope, as a
defensive response to government (and potentially populist) intervention.

Subsequently, if "cyber-streets" are "patrolled" by capitalist institutions, rather than by the government or communitarian groups, it will
inevitably become more difficult "to turn the one-way system of commercial media into a two-way process of discussion, reflection, and action" (Thoman, 1998). As Paul Resnick (1997) explains, no matter how
well conceived or executed, any labeling or blocking system will tend
to stifle noncommercial communication since the time and energy
needed to label will inevitably lead to many unlabeled sites:

> Because of safety concerns, some people will block access to ma-
> terials that are unlabeled or whose labels are untrusted. For such
> people, the Internet will function more like broadcasting, provid-
> ing access only to sites with sufficient mass-market appeal to
> merit the cost of labeling. (p. 69)

This is a serious problem, as the possibilities for a decentralization of
information will once again be delimited by a top-down capitalist hierarchy wherein nondominant, noncommercial, or alternative sources
of information will remain peripheral. As Lewis (1996) explains, "Microsoft's implementation of the filtering system would give parents the
options of blocking access to *any* Web material without a RSACi rating"
(emphasis added).

Consequently, the need for better, concrete proposals for inquiry-
based learning will be presented in the next chapter. Within my model,
the issues of ownership, profit, control, and related effects are essential
to helping students formulate constructive action ideas that will lead
to their own Internet choices and surfing habits as well as local, national, or global action. If we are going to relinquish the power of labeling, ratings, and restrictions to a third party, then we need to make
sure that they are working on behalf of our *public* interests, rather than
private, commercial interests. This is especially important as schools
are looking to these products and services as solutions to "inappropri-

ate" content, rather than as part of the problem. What complicates these measures is the fact that such products disable children or students from discerning the kind of information or material they come across, evaluating the benefits of the acquired information to other forms of media or research tools, or deciding for themselves what is or isn't appropriate.

Len Masterman's explanation of critical autonomy (1985), to "develop in pupils enough self-confidence and critical maturity to be able to apply critical judgements to media texts *which they will encounter in their future*" (p. 24), does not fit within the logic of software blocking systems or even adult monitoring. As Elizabeth Thoman (1998) clarifies, the media "have become so ingrained in our cultural milieu that we should no longer view the task of media education as providing 'protection' against unwanted messages." Hence a learning model of awareness, analysis, reflection, action, and experience leads to better comprehension, critical thinking, and informed judgments (Thoman, 1998). As PICS chairman Paul Resnick admits, "no labeling system is a full substitute for a thorough and thoughtful evaluation" (1997, p. 64). In the end, while I disagree with the products and rationale of SafeSurf, Net Nanny, and CyberPatrol, I do agree with these Web entities on one thing: "There is more to be gained than just the free flow of information."

## NOTES

1. This is not to say that the issue of regulation could not lead to important policies that protect Internet users from dangerous or improper sites, but that efforts to determine and regulate such material nevertheless remain political, and deserve careful thought.

2. Clearly, no one can ignore the fact that age is directly related to one's ability to foresee the dangers of accessing certain sites. Thus there are many reputable initiatives designed to deter or redirect young students/children from unsuitable material.

3. Disney is cognizant of the extensive "power of advertising" in ensnaring adults as easily as kids. I admit to clicking onto Disney's ad link for HomePoint.com, one of the largest online home furniture catalogues. Interestingly enough, the celebrity endorser for the virtual store was making a debut on Disney's television network station ABC.

4. Microsystems Software is a private company that develops and markets various software products. In 1995, Microsystems ranked 223rd on the Inc. 500 list of the fastest-growing privately held companies.

**5** _____

# The Limits and Benefits of Technology Initiatives in Massachusetts Schools

This chapter describes the results of the content analysis and assessment of various technological initiatives devised, implemented, and funded in Massachusetts schools. Beginning with a description of the Lighthouse Technology Grants, the first part of the chapter explains how each of the projects funded through state allocations was conceptualized and categorized according to subject area. The findings of this study are summarized in the next part of the chapter. Through tables, a description of the various projects funded through the grants is provided for each of the subject categories, explaining what kinds of learning initiatives emanated from classroom projects and activities. The implications of these findings account for the final part of the chapter. Through the theoretical models offered by Benjamin S. Bloom et al. (1956), Roger Osborne and Peter Freyberg (1985), and John D. Bransford and Nancy J. Vye (1989), I'll demonstrate the need for a media literacy curriculum by presenting the limitations and oversights of the technology projects taking place in Massachusetts schools.

## LIGHTHOUSE TECHNOLOGY GRANTS

Financed through the federal Technology Literacy Challenge Fund, the Lighthouse Technology Grants are designed to identify, enhance, and disseminate existing classroom projects that incorporate new technologies with the learning standards of the Massachusetts state curriculum frameworks in a way that is innovative and motivates students to learn. For the 1998–1999 school year, 173 proposals were received and 74 Lighthouse Technology Grants were awarded, totaling $1,987,387.

By examining a complete listing of the grants administered in the 1998–1999 academic school year through the Massachusetts Department of Education, all 74 of the grant recipients and their projects implemented across the curriculum were analyzed and evaluated. Each of the funded school projects was categorized according to subject area, namely language arts, technology, science, social studies, math, business, art/graphic design, music, special education (SPED), English as a second language (ESL), foreign language, interdisciplinary programs, and assessment. Some school programs did not fall neatly within these categories because they offered skills in more than one subject area. Consequently, some grant recipients were cross-listed under more than one subject heading. Although all of the subject categories draw from technological programs or applications, those units specifically focused on technology as a subject were categorized separately under the technology category.

Within each classification, each grant project was listed according to its central theme or design. Appendix A provides a detailed description of each of the funded projects within the listed subjects. For the purposes of this chapter, the grant activities were summarized into tables to simplify the cross-listing of projects under several subject areas. Although similar projects were grouped together, each of the funded programs represents different schools from across the state.

### Research Findings

The first observation in the examination of the Lighthouse Technology Grants was that the funded projects and activities were not limited to any particular subject area. As outlined in Table 5.1, the largest amount of technology projects fell under the language arts category, with a total of fourteen sponsored activities. Twelve projects were funded in science and thirteen across disciplines. Projects specifically focused on technology totaled nine, while there were eight in social studies, six in math, four in business, four in art/graphic design, two in music, and two in foreign language. In addition to these core subject areas, two of the grants were used as assessment tools, two for special education, and one for English as a second language.

Table 5.2 provides a summary of the various projects funded within language arts. Among the fourteen projects, nine of them focused on enhancing student reading and writing or promoting literacy skills by having students use software programs to help improve grammar, organization, sequence, and research.

**Table 5.1**
**Lighthouse Technology Grants**

| Subject Area | Number of Projects |
|---|---|
| Language arts | 14 |
| Technology | 9 |
| Science | 12 |
| Social studies | 8 |
| Math | 6 |
| Business | 4 |
| Art/graphic design | 4 |
| Music | 2 |
| Special education | 2 |
| ESL | 1 |
| Foreign language | 2 |
| Interdisciplinary | 13 |
| Assessment | 2 |

**Table 5.2**
**Lighthouse Technology Grants: Language Arts**

| |
|---|
| Enhanced reading and writing through computer software |
| Hyperstudio presentations |
| Verbal literacy through alternative methods |
| Online student magazines |
| Language arts / social studies ancestry unit |
| Video technology used to write for a specific audience |
| Publishing books and drawings |
| Web-based research and data collection on children's literature |
| Power Point presentation slides based on language arts research |

**Table 5.3**
**Lighthouse Technology Grants: Technology**

| |
|---|
| *Sim City 2000* simulation software for State curriculum unit on cities |
| Maintenance of school district Web site and teacher/student internship training to publish on Internet |
| Biotechnology, lasers, telecommunications, and environmental technology |
| Research, data collection, problem solving, communicating ideas, and discourse with other students and professionals |
| Industry standard drafting software for architectural styles, structure, and neighborhood development |

Hardware components, such as computer scanners, were used to publish books and illustrations. Hyperstudio, Kid Pix, WiggleWorks, and AVID cinema desktop video were among the computer programs used to integrate language arts curriculum with technology. Specifically, these programs allowed students to (a) organize presentations relating to topics from the language arts curriculum designed to integrate with technology, (b) create individual slides based on research projects in language arts, (c) acquire early literacy and produce their own books, and (d) create original work and speak and write clearly for a specific audience. Other projects included an online student magazine, Internet connections and CD-ROMs for a language arts/social studies unit, and Web-site access for elementary school teachers using children's literature for multicultural discussions. Altogether, these projects aimed to teach students to become proficient readers and writers.

While all of the projects integrated technology into their subject areas, there were some activities that focused specifically on the development of skills in technology. As represented in Table 5.3, these projects included the use of software programs, such as Sim City 2000, a simulation software designed to meet state curriculum standards on cities, and computer-aided drafting (CAD) architectural design, an industry standard drafting software program enabling students to better understand architectural styles, structure, and neighborhood development. A technology grant also enabled the maintenance of a school district Web site and the training of teachers and students to use the Internet as a publishing tool. In addition to the funding of technology projects aligned with state curriculum standards for industrial and language arts, research in biotechnology, lasers, telecommunications, and environmental technology were affiliated with science standards.

**Table 5.4**
**Lighthouse Technology Grants: Science**

| |
|---|
| Machines built and programmed with LEGO/DACTA software |
| Physics--force, motion, energy, light, sound--taught with technology and math concepts |
| Species and habitats data collected and shared online through e-mail, bulletin boards |
| Scientific investigations of local water samples |
| Outdoor environments and ecosystems studies, also associated to area histories |
| Physics of sailing, hydro- and aerodynamics, ocean ecology, and world cultures |

Many of the Lighthouse Grants went to fund projects in science. Table 5.4 summarizes some of the activities representing the grants. Various computer technologies were employed to conduct experiments in physics and mathematics, aerodynamics, and ecology. For instance, middle school students at one school used technology to study the physics of sailing, hydro- and aerodynamics, ocean ecology, and world cultures through a ten-month program. Students at another school researched species and habitats through online data collection, graphing calculators, e-mail, bulletin boards, and other applications. Data collection, writing, summaries, and electronic presentations accompanied many of these science activities. Technology was central to each of these projects, as it enabled students to understand difficult concepts, test samples, and share information with others through newspapers, video portfolios, computers, Web pages, and e-mail.

In the area of social studies, Internet technology was used to allow classrooms to access government and historical materials, Web-based curricular materials, relevant information, and other classrooms in order to exchange and compare collected data (see Table 5.5). For example, one class used Web-based curriculum materials designed by teachers and museum professionals to exhibit a cyber–history museum. As with most of the funded projects, other computer applications were utilized to create databases, newspapers, video portfolios, Web pages, or presentations.

Only a handful of projects in mathematics were funded through the Lighthouse Grants. Two of the projects categorized under math were cross-listed and previously described under science. Accordingly, the activities listed in Table 5.6 describe technological applications for data

**Table 5.5**
**Lighthouse Technology Grants: Social Studies**

| |
| --- |
| Internet access to government and historical materials |
| "History Museum" designed through Web-based curriculum materials |
| Internet "information hunt" to student-generated questions relating to new historical or literary units |
| Multimedia approach to studying and presenting history of Ipswich |
| Database collection and electronic exchange of data on Massachusetts geography, government, history and economy |
| Technology used to research black inventors |

**Table 5.6**
**Lighthouse Technology Grants: Math**

| |
| --- |
| Biodiversity data collection |
| Student-designed and -constructed interactive math Web sites |
| Computer math games and software programs to teach and reinforce math skills |

collection, the design and construction of interactive math Web sites, and the use of computer software programs and games to help teach and reinforce math skills.

Providing experience and courses in business, the grants represented in Table 5.7 document projects that allowed students to be matched with mentors from local businesses through e-mail communication software, and to complete design projects using state-of-the-art design techniques for clients from the business communities in their school districts. For example, the "Key Pal Community and Business Connections for Middle Grades" paired students with business mentors on curriculum-based projects aligned with state frameworks. Additionally, high school seniors used technology to build a portfolio of their work experiences from a five-week "School-to-Work" internship program and prepare electronic slideshow presentations about their learned skills to share with other students. The final project allowed twelfth-grade students to use the latest technology to research investment options, create and maintain portfolios, track the performance of markets and companies, and participate in an online stock market investment game.

**Table 5.7**
**Lighthouse Technology Grants: Business**

| |
|---|
| "Key Pal Community and Business Connections" |
| Electronic portfolio of five-week job internship program |
| Design projects created for business-community clients |
| Online research of investment options, portfolio creation, and participation in stock market investment game |

**Table 5.8**
**Lighthouse Technology Grants: Art/Graphic Design and Music**

| |
|---|
| Internet access, research, and writing documentation of artists and art movements |
| Logo creation and marketing package for imaginary client |
| Graphic arts applications, such as resolution, color separation, file formats, and various media outputs |
| "Music Technology Lab" for learning composition, transcribing, and basics of musical notation |
| Known and original works digitized and combined by visual arts and music students |

Although art/graphic design and music were separately categorized, Table 5.8 represents the two subject areas together. Subsequently, technology enabled students to research artists whose work is displayed at the Boston Museum of Fine Arts, and allowed music and visual arts students to digitize known and original works. Graphic arts technology provided students with the tools to learn to produce a logo and marketing package for an imaginary client using researched art styles. A "Music Technology Lab" allowed students in grades nine through twelve to learn the elements of composition, transcribing and musical notation, ear training, and rhythm.

After language arts, the largest number of Lighthouse Technology Grants were interdisciplinary (see Table 5.9). Internet access and navigation was central to the development of projects based on research and data collection for multidisciplinary programs and special topics on multiculturalism, geography, ancient history, literature, inspirational figures, and the Iditarod dogsled race. E-mail was also central to

**Table 5.9**
**Lighthouse Technology Grants: Interdisciplinary Programs**

| |
| --- |
| "Virtual High School" course offerings through the Internet/ email |
| Internet and multimedia for research and written essays |
| School Web site publishing of stories, poetry, science projects, maps, and artwork |
| Computer work stations, video, and Internet used for Multidisciplinary subjects |
| Hyperstudio audiovisual presentations and research projects |
| Live video conferencing with Walpole senior citizens for Interdisciplinary social studies unit |
| Infomercials produced on Ware's TV channel 3 and in-house access station |
| Project Challenge Lab for high school students with special needs, in foster care, or at risk |

**Table 5.10**
**Lighthouse Technology Grants: Foreign Language/ESL**

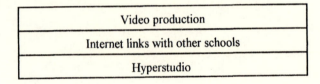

| |
| --- |
| Video production |
| Internet links with other schools |
| Hyperstudio |

activities involving electronic exchanges with teachers, other students, or educational organizations. For instance, one school participates in the "Virtual High School," where students learn in a technology-rich environment while participating in courses offered over the Internet. Other projects utilized technology to produce "infomercials" for cable access channels, tutor special-needs or at-risk students, create portfolios, and enable live video conferencing.

Table 5.10 represents funded projects in the teaching of foreign languages and English as a second language. Such programs allowed K–12 students in one school to produce videos primarily in a foreign language using research, scripts, storyboards, video cameras, audio mix-

**Table 5.11**
**Lighthouse Technology Grants: Special Education**

| Multisensory learning |
|---|
| Video editing |

**Table 5.12**
**Lighthouse Technology Grants: Assessment**

| Videotaped presentations and interviews |
|---|
| Interactive CD-ROM-based multimedia |

ers, VCRs, and computer editing software. It also provided students with electronic access to other schools in the United States and Vietnam in order to develop instructional materials and improve communication and subject area skills. Hyperstudio was used in another school to help ESL students develop their English vocabulary.

The first of two Lighthouse Grants designated to special-education programs (see Table 5.11) provided multisensory learning opportunities for special-needs and non-special-needs students in prekindergarten, kindergarten, and elementary classrooms. The second grant was used to enable deaf and hard-of-hearing students to work collaboratively with hearing students to produce and direct the production of videos using special software and hardware to edit and create the final captioned videos.

The final category of projects, outlined in Table 5.12, utilized technology to support and disseminate student assessment practices. One of the grants in this category allowed second-grade students to reflect on and direct their own learning, and helped teachers improve their classroom instruction in math and reading. Students used videotaped presentations and interviews as part of their portfolios. The second grant used interactive CD-ROM–based multimedia portfolios as an ongoing assessment and individual curriculum planning tool.

## Implications

Throughout my review of the descriptive summaries of the projects, I was not only interested in discovering the multiple ways in which technology was being incorporated into various subject areas, but was also searching for models offering a critical media literacy approach, encouraging students to reflect on technological forms, benefits and drawbacks, ownership, access, informational accuracy, visual design, and so forth. My hope was that I would find some strategies, lesson plans, or ideas that would enhance the development of a media literacy curriculum in cyberspace. However, the results of my analysis confirmed that no critical media literacy approaches were applied to the use of new telecommunications technology through the Lighthouse Grants.

Using the major categories of Bloom's cognitive domain of the taxonomy of educational objectives (1956) (see Appendix B), the Lighthouse Grants focused primarily on knowledge, comprehension, and application. Students used technology to reinforce previously learned skills or material through the use of software programs, computer games, CD-ROMs, or materials available over the Internet. In order to grasp the meaning of material and translate it from one form to another, students used technology to present a story, project, or assignment through multisensory media. Most of the application occurred through the use of computer labs, video equipment, and multimedia programs such as Hyperstudio.

As for the higher levels of learning within Bloom's taxonomy, namely analysis, synthesis, and evaluation, most of the projects did not develop into a rigorous methodology combining the deconstruction, (re)production, and critical judgment of the information or material provided by the technology. Osborne and Freyberg (1985) summarize research on the methods of achieving critical thinking, which include activities or situations that challenge students' initial ideas through a series of "What if" questions. Such questions are used to stimulate thinking about the consequences of students' initial ideas. This phase is aligned with Bloom's analytical component, which encourages students to identify, question, and recognize the organizational principles involved in the learning material. This essential phase of learning went largely undeveloped within the grants, as students weren't always given opportunities to contrast their initial ideas and strategies with other possibilities or alternatives. Bransford and Vye (1989) specify the importance of problem-solving exercises/activities that allow students to see how new knowledge affects their own perception and comprehension and relates to a variety of situations. Such problem-solving exercises were not central to the curricular assignments and activities funded through the grants.

Consequently, although the types of projects funded were fairly creative in their utilization of technology, the content did not radically deviate from a non-technology-based curriculum. This is especially evident in the area of language arts, where none of the grant-funded programs approached the critical components established within the Massachusetts curriculum standards for English language arts. While the projects did abide by standards for the use of a variety of electronic media for research or data collection, such as computerized card catalogs, online databases, and electronic almanacs and encyclopedias, the higher levels of critical learning standards were not developed.

Specifically, I'm referring to the standards calling for (1) the comparison and contrast of each medium and its variant informational perspective, (2) the selection and quality evaluation of appropriate electronic media obtained, (3) the identification of techniques used in television (and other media) and use of knowledge to distinguish between facts and misleading information, (4) the analysis of reader/viewer emotive response to text and image in print journalism, images, text, and sound in electronic journalism, distinguishing the techniques used in each to achieve these effects, (5) the analysis and evaluation of techniques used in a media message for a particular audience, and (6) the identification and evaluation of aesthetic effects and techniques used to create a media presentation. Hence most of the grant projects in language arts that used technology to enhance literacy, the writing process, and basic research skills never allowed the next cognitive levels of learning within these standards to evolve.

Not only were programs in language arts lacking in their development of higher-level thinking models, but other subject areas were equally deficient in their design, as they did not meet the analytical or evaluative learning criteria within Bloom's taxonomy. For instance, in science/social studies, the use of technology to research black inventors did not address key questions relating to *why* such inventors remain marginalized within historical literature or culture. In art, the selection process and representativeness of the work displayed at the Boston Museum of Fine Arts was not directly interrogated. The electronic data collection and exchange of information on Massachusetts government, history, and economy wasn't focused on raising issues concerning equity, justice, or power. Instead, these multidisciplinary projects offering "the latest technology" merely change the nature of informational acquisition rather than the purpose of the learning venture.

Among the state standards calling for the design and creation of coherent media production, the grants better approached the frameworks for the creation of age-appropriate media productions for presentations and broadcast or electronic transmission. However, the projects do not go far enough in connecting media production with personal experience, perspective, social and political public issues, and action.

This is not to say that some of the projects did not attempt to incorporate critical media literacy components into their grants. Nevertheless, these efforts were limited to two and were insufficient. One language arts program encouraged students to evaluate and make choices about the various types of media available to them, namely books, magazines, television, radio, computers, and the Internet. For instance, students seeking information for a book report would be better informed about the kinds of resources available through books, newspapers, and the Internet. Yet this approach fell short of encouraging a systematic look at how specific media choices impact viewer/reader/listener comprehension; it privileged an individual rather than sociocultural analysis. A second interdisciplinary program prepared sixth-graders with research skills combining note-taking with information literacy skills. However, the project did not aim to enhance competencies in critical informational discernment through analytical or evaluative projects. Instead, it offered Hyperstudio audiovisual presentations as a technological means through which to organize information for parents and other students based on interdisciplinary content materials.

Accordingly, my findings indicate that the Lighthouse Grants did not encourage students to reflect upon and judge (analyze and evaluate) the veracity and sociopolitical implications of the materials acquired through telecommunications technology, CD-ROMs, software programs, or computer games. Furthermore, the utilization of video and multimedia capabilities to produce media did not radically alter (or synthesize) the content of the materials being presented, but simply enhanced the form through which it was (re)presented. Consequently, confusion about technology's purpose, in the classroom as well as in the curriculum, is reflected in the activities and design of the Lighthouse Grants. Further research in the assessment and evaluation of these grant projects is needed to discover if and how the use of communication tools leads to critical learning achievements.

## ADDITIONAL MASSACHUSETTS TECHNOLOGICAL INITIATIVES

The Lighthouse Technology Grants are not the only Educational Technology ("EdTech") initiatives funded by the state of Massachusetts. Two other programs have been financially backed by the Massachusetts Department of Education (DOE).

### VHS: Virtual High School

The first EdTech program to receive funding is the Virtual High School (VHS) project. Funded by the U.S. Department of Education "Technology Innovation Challenge Grant" in October 1996, the Virtual High School project creates and conveys academic content via the Internet. The Massachusetts grant recipients at Hudson Public Schools and the Concord Consortium describe how virtual schools collaborate with other high schools from across the country to offer their students "NetCourses" ranging from advanced academic courses to technical and specialized courses. Virtual schools supply computers, Internet connections, staff time, and a site coordinator who is responsible for managing and supporting teachers and students within the school. In order to provide high-quality instruction, class size is limited to twenty students for each NetCourse, and teachers enroll in the Teachers Learning Conference, a graduate-level NetCourse that offers participants effective educational strategies and technologies.

With eighty-eight schools across the United States currently participating in the project, the array of courses offered for credit on the Internet is continually expanding. Beginning in 1996, sixty Massachusetts teachers were involved in the VHS program, which is coordinated by the Concord Consortium. The number of participating teachers will increase dramatically when more teachers complete the twenty-six-week training session and go online.

Among some of the positive feedback offered by VHS teachers and students is an expressed optimism that the project offers students an opportunity that they would otherwise never have in small schools with limited course offerings. Teachers and administrators looking at educational reform believe that the VHS project provides an alternative way to reach students other than the four walls of the classroom. This enthusiasm is shared by students who are learning-disabled or forced to stay at home for medical reasons, as the program allows them to overcome difficulties presented by traditional classrooms.

Along with student, teacher, and administrative accolades, several scholars would endorse the VHS program as an effective use of technology in education. As previously cited in the literature review, New Zealand scholars Lalita Rajasingham and John Tiffin (1995) were among the first to propose educational reform in an information society through "telecourses" offered in virtual schools or colleges. Because the "telestudent" is no longer confined by space or time, Rajasingham and Tiffin celebrate the independence of the learner. Their companions would include George Landow (1992), Richard Lanham (1993), and Jay David Bolter (1991), all of whom applaud the "more democratic, learner-centered, holistic, and natural" processes of working with new electronic media. Likewise, scholars of critical pedagogy, such as Colin Lankshear, Michael Peters, and Michele Knobel (1996), would align themselves with optimists who see the potential for these technologies to radically alter classroom dynamics by displacing traditional teacher-centered pedagogy, encouraging participation, and offering flexible schedules.

In spite of these favorable evaluations, my reservations about the Virtual High School remain founded in my earlier criticism, as programs such as these do not necessarily alter or enrich the learning objectives. They further extend the technological possibilities or *means* of education without radically altering the *content*. As such, online class activity resembles the face-to-face class in many ways. The teacher still organizes the course materials and determines the progression, while students respond to individual or group assignments. What remains to be determined is how virtual courses can enhance higher cognitive aptitudes through creative collaborative ventures that question, analyze, and evaluate subject matter through critical learning.

### YTE: Youth Tech Entrepreneurs

The second DOE EdTech program is the Youth Tech Entrepreneurs (YTE). The goal of the program is to create student technology leaders in Massachusetts public schools by having high school students maintain schools' computer systems, run technology workshops, and develop high-tech businesses. According to the DOE, the bedrock of the YTE program is its project-based curriculum, where students learn by taking leading roles in real-life projects at their schools and in their communities. They teach other young students, work with faculty and staff to maintain computer networks, and provide technology support services to community businesses.

As high school sophomores, YTE students begin their commitment to participate in the program for three years. Although the selection of students for the project is not described, those students accepted into the program are required to attend YTE classes as an academic requirement during the school day and must also attend monthly labs on Saturdays and volunteer for after-school technology-based projects. Through partnerships with local businesses and individual adult mentors, YTE offers paid and unpaid summer internships. Courses for YTE are based on the Massachusetts Curricular Frameworks with a focus on the student acquisition of skills in problem solving, writing, presentation, and leadership.

As technicians, YTE students are taught to repair and maintain computer systems. By the end of the first academic year, students must take the "A+ Certification Exam," a rigorous and respected industry standard test. In their second and third years, students develop skills in computer training. As teachers, students learn to teach others what they have learned. During their first year, students run workshops on how to use computers more effectively at home and in the classroom. Finally, as entrepreneurs, students develop innovative projects that serve their communities; they create and run help centers at their school, provide free home Internet access for district students, and build computers for themselves and their teachers.

Despite the DOE's enthusiasm and commitment to the Youth Tech Entrepreneurs and its anticipated success, the program's focus and educational thrust must be carefully examined. Ultimately, the DOE extols the program's goal of filling the void of 300,000 technology jobs in the United States upon the successful completion of the certification test. This presents many conceptual and practical problems with the program. First, the DOE does not specify what the "industry standards" for the certification exam entail, which means it's hard to know precisely what kind of learning skills are taught throughout the program. Going back to Bloom's taxonomy, the skills emphasized within the YTE program are based on the lower tiers of cognitive learning—knowledge and application—because students are merely taught to learn and apply, rather than reorganize, current uses of technology.

This issue is further complicated by the use of students as an inexpensive labor force. Although the state clearly benefits from technology-proficient students because they can help overcome the odds of one computer troubleshooter for every 700 teachers and students, many objections can be raised about educational training programs or learning curricula based on money-saving, and essentially profitable, state and private business practices. As *New York Times* writer Pamela Mendels (1998) explains, the YTE program is "part of a small but growing number of educational institutions across the country that are training students in computer skills, and then using them to help reduce the heavy labor costs associated with running school computer systems":

> The trend spotlights a problem faced by school districts that have opted to offer cutting-edge computer courses and systems in a bid to satisfy everyone from demanding parents to White House officials who tout the educational advantages of the Internet. In a nutshell, computer-laden school districts, like corporations, are finding that they increasingly require information systems departments to help solve computer problems and Internet glitches. But unlike businesses, many schools don't have the money to pay for technical support. So, enter the student trainees.

For Mendels, the problems presented by such technology programs are that they rely too heavily on affordable student trainees, which risks "over-stressing the young people and missing out on the benefits of an experienced professional computer staff." These considerations are further exacerbated by a fundamental question: Who gets to determine the learning outcomes or objectives of such technological programs? It's clear that the business community has a stake in setting the agenda of such programs, as they will in turn be provided with skilled student interns or future employees. This helps explain why sponsorship for the 1998 pilot program at Malden High School included seed money from the Harbus Foundation, an enterprise based at the student newspaper of the Harvard Business School, as well as provisions from the Mass Networks Education Partnership, an independent, nonprofit organization of people from education, business, government, and labor working to promote the use of information and communication technology as a tool for education reform. Whether it be through independent or private organizations, this shift toward educational reform begs the question: Reform for whom? The reality is that most curricular reform is driven by the values, practices, and imperatives of the marketplace or business community, thereby promoting practical skills rather than higher levels of cognitive thinking skills essential to independent learning. This is why "the theories, policies, and practices involved in education are not technical . . . they are inherently ethical and political" (Apple, 1990, cited in Sholle & Denski, 1994, p. 3).

There are many educational scholars who find a market-driven technology program disconcerting. Henry Giroux and Peter McLaren (1989) problematize curricular designs that organize classroom learning within an institutional context specifying a particular version of "what knowledge is of most worth, in what direction we should desire, and what it means to know something" because they realize that the process of selecting what to teach students is extremely political (p. 239). As Ira Shor (1992) reiterates, "socialization and curriculum are political processes of inclusion and exclusion; that is, what people learn to believe, say, want, and do presupposes other knowledge and choices left out of their development" (p. 119). Shor notes that the political and economic systems dominated by elite products, language, perceptions, and policies are reflected in a mass culture and traditional curriculum that encourage student passivity and little to no investment in the learning process.

For these reasons, Peter McLaren (1988) has advanced a critical pedagogy "founded on the conviction that schooling for self and social empowerment is ethically prior to a mastery of technical skills" (cited in Scholle & Denski, 1994, p. 24). This does not mean that students must work individually in order to reach a level of empowerment, but that students need to learn more than marketable skills in order to become critically engaged with their personal, communal, and cultural environments. In considering the political and economic curricular terrains affecting school reform, Paulo Freire (1989) offers a useful distinction between schooling and education: Schooling is primarily a form of social control in which the forms of pedagogy normalize subjects to take up places as skilled citizens in the given social order. Education serves as a form of potential transformation in which the forms of pedagogy allow for active subjects committed to self- and social empowerment (cited in Sholle & Denski, 1994, p. 26).

Subsequently, if Freire's notion of "educational empowerment" is to occur within state-funded technological programs, such as YTE, the integration of technology and learning must go beyond a mastery of computer skills or proficiencies. By developing skills in critical analysis, synthesis, and evaluation, students should be led to ask whose interests are being served or challenged through the use of particular technology and what are their own commitments to such practices. This would allow them to master the skills needed to gain knowledge throughout life rather than prompting them to acquire a set of technological "skills" or "facts" divorced from an understanding of how and why those skills/facts were acquired.

## PLANNING AHEAD: CONCEPTUALIZING A TECHNOLOGY-BASED LITERACY PROGRAM

In conceptualizing the overall curriculum for a technology-based literacy program, the following principles of critical pedagogy and education should be kept in mind.[1] First, "the curriculum must develop in dialogue with the concerns of students"—not just predefined career needs, but "the conscious and unconscious critical thoughts and feelings that surface in students' everyday lives." This approach encourages self-motivated learning for personal rather than merely economic ends, and prepares students to act as citizens who question knowledge and society. Second, "a narrow vocationalism should be rejected" (no job tracks), as this privileges a market-driven schooling model rather than an educational empowerment model. Third, "theory and practice must be integrated in all classwork and outside experiences" so that students are allowed to conceptualize and utilize technology in new and creative ways (synthesis) at school and elsewhere (Sholle and Denski, 1994, p. 157). This helps to prepare students to invest in their own learning through new technological forms that will only become more pervading with time. Fourth, no classroom arrangements should dictate the structure of the technology curriculum (past enrollment models, job-track mechanism, weed-out courses, time-bound structures). Students should be allowed to offer and follow their own learning directions in equal-opportunity classrooms where all students have access to computer technology and are properly guided and encouraged by teachers and administrators. Fifth, the forms of technology that impact students' lives should be given primary focus without artificially separating privileged forms of technology from devalued forms. Shor (1992) suggests that teachers should research students in order to discover, integrate, and address their language and issues. Acknowledgment of student culture does not mean that students know all they need to know or that teachers don't know anything special, for teacher knowledge is crucial to the transformative process (p. 202); but the learning of new technology should be inclusive of various technological forms and content. Finally, the curriculum should address pedagogy itself so that the classroom is viewed not only as a site of instruction, but also "as a cultural arena, that is, as a site of cultural struggle in which various sociological and ideological struggles" related to technology "are continually being played out" (Sholle & Denski, 1994, p. 23).

Such a curriculum would encourage students to develop knowledge of (a) the sorts of choices available in the production, processes, and uses of technology, and (b) the effects or influences these choices hold over their understanding, uses, and interpretation of technology, and would provide them with (c) the analytical ability to recognize and deal with these choices wisely, both as creators of and respondents to technological forms.

Consequently, serious thought must be devoted to the development of technology curricula across subject areas in ways that encourage systematic analysis, interrogation, and evaluation. The lack of grants directed at offering higher levels of critical learning *with* and *about* technology further necessitate the need for the conceptualization and implementation of a technology-based media literacy curriculum. Although the scope of this book does not allow for the development of media literacy lessons and activities for all technological forms and subject areas, the following chapter will offer some essential foundations leading to the construction of critical frameworks.

## NOTE

1. These principles are adaptations from David Sholle and Stan Denski's work on media education models in the text *Media Education and the (Re)production of Culture* (1994).

# 6

## Empowerment over Censorship: Using Media Literacy in Cyberspace

Among the various conceptualizations informing the use of technology in the classroom, we've learned that Massachusetts students are taught a variety of computer literacy skills ranging from computer technology and operation, storyboarding, programing techniques, and data acquisition, to word-processing, software applications, and publishing. What remains absent from these learning activities and lessons are critical literacy skills allowing students to reflect on and question the underlying structures, content, and elements of computer and technological applications. The shortage of curricular designs and classroom lessons equipped to teach such critical skills plays a contributing role in the dearth of technology-related teaching models. Aimee Dorr and Craig Brannon (1992) explain that although there has been a rash of books with suggestions on how to teach about computers, most include suggestions for teaching about the technology—input/output devices, bits and bytes, printing, and the like—through basic instruction about how the technology works and how to interact with it. Only some include programming, while virtually all include many suggestions about how to use the technology to carry out routine educational activities such as learning mathematics, doing research for a paper, managing data from a science experiment, and writing poetry (p. 91). Essentially, few books and resources exist that espouse a critical understanding of technology.

Similar to the results found in the research of Dorr and Brannon, our analysis of the Lighthouse Grants confirms that the use of computers as an alternate means to deliver a lesson is education *with*, not *about*, the computer (p. 91). This disconcerting educational emphasis is exacerbated by studies indicating that most teacher training in technology is weak and "tends to ignore concepts such as visual literacy, critical viewing skills, and media education," despite the fact that the concepts are now more than thirty years old (Considine, 1990, cited in Dorr & Brannon, pp. 29–30). In a study conducted by Main and Roberts (1990), between 50 percent and 91 percent of California teachers surveyed said that staff development was needed in integrating computers into the curriculum (cited in Dorr & Brannon, p. 94). Dorr and Brannon cite further research indicating that when it comes to computers, the majority of teachers do not feel highly competent. This level of discomfort with computer technology is further increased with the emergence of new information technologies. As David Buckingham (1998) warns, "these technologies are regarded by some as an educational panacea":

> Like television in an earlier era, there is a risk that they [new digital technologies] will be seen as merely neutral and instrumental, as simply teaching aids. In this context, it is vital to insist on the critical questions, for example, about agency and representation with which media educators have traditionally been concerned. The key aspects of media education provide a framework that can productively be applied to these new media and that takes us beyond a superficial infatuation with technology for its own sake. (pp. 33–34)

Subsequently, media literacy skills need to be devised across subject and curriculum areas so that the study of media and technology include the systematic analysis of the social, political, ethical, and economic aspects of these communication forms. The intersecting educational strands of computer literacy, information literacy, and digital literacy need to be reconfigured in order to form an overarching matrix connecting the distinct parameters of technology curricula.

## MULTIPLE MEDIA LITERACIES

Using Joshua Meyrowitz's concept of "multiple media literacies" (1998), as well as institutional media analysis, there are four phases or types of media literacy that need to be considered in designing an effective technology curriculum. The first type of media literacy perceives the media as conduits that carry messages. As Meyrowitz explains, this understanding of media leads to a set of questions, approaches, and research focused on media *content* literacy, whereby the ability to access and analyze media messages or content becomes the underlying organizational catalyst of media literacy. This content-based approach is easily transferable from one medium to another, as the elements of study in this model examine how meaning is created through various forms, whether it be books, newspapers, television, radio, or Internet Web pages. Specifically, content skills require

> being able to decode and follow the intended manifest message; exploring intended and unintended latent messages; being aware of different content genres; being aware of the cultural, institutional, and commercial forces that tend to lead to certain types of messages being constructed while others are avoided; and understanding that different individuals and groups tend to "read" the same "texts" differently. (p. 97)

Although media content literacy is the most prominent method of studying the media, Meyrowitz contends that this approach does not delimit the essential competencies that should accompany media literacy: "when content is the focus, not much attention tends to be given to the particular characteristics of the medium through which the messages examined are conveyed" (p. 99). Another way of studying the media is to examine each distinctive "grammar" or language of a medium. Media *grammar* literacy focuses on the distinct grammar of each medium. For instance, the language used to convey meaning through television/film is organized through camera pans, cuts, zooms, fades, close-ups, and the like. This conceptual understanding of media as languages emerges from the analysis and evaluation of production variables used within each medium to shape perception and response to mediated communications. By manipulating some of the communication variables in a particular form, such as editing a televised program to create a new narrative or making collages out of magazines, students can learn to alter perceptions of message content. As Meyrowitz explains, computer programs and Web sites are increasingly incorporating many of the variables of text, photography, sound, and motion to create message content. While these variables are shared by other media, the languages of each medium are unique and affect how meaning is communicated through these variables.

In accordance with Meyrowitz's explanation of the grammar variables characteristic of media forms, the New London Group—an international group of scholars who believe in the integration of literacy theory, electronic literacy tools, and constructivist pedagogy—has similarly emphasized the importance of understanding the design elements that compose different modes of meaning. Linguistic, audio, visual, spatial, gestural, and multimodal elements comprise the metalanguages describing and interpreting a design for multi-literacies (Tyner, 1998).

Within visual modes of meaning, students learn to analyze and manipulate elements of visual meaning, such as colors, perspective, vectors, foreground and background, and the like. Audio design would constitute elements of music, sound effects, emotive response, and so forth. Elements of linguistic meaning include delivery, vocabulary and metaphor, modality, transitivity, normalization of processes, information structure, and local and global coherence relations. These are among some of the design elements informing curricular models aiming to expand the modes of representation more broadly than language alone. This multi-literacies design also creates a pedagogy whereby "language and other modes of meaning are seen as dynamic representational resources, constantly being remade by their users as they work to achieve their various cultural purposes" (New London Group, 1996, cited in Tyner, 1998, p. 80).

The final conception of media accounted for in Meyrowitz's multi-literacies is *medium* literacy, which examines how the specific traits of a medium set it apart from other communication contexts and interactions. Stemming from Marshall McLuhan's medium theory (1964), Meyrowitz (1998) explains the importance of analyzing how the characteristics of a specific medium alter communication, "both on the micro-, single-situation level and on the macro-, societal level" (p. 103). For example:

> microlevel medium literacy . . . could entail understanding why a particular type of interaction (e.g., contacting someone for a date, ending an intimate relationship, inquiring about a job, selling a particular product, negotiating a peace treaty, etc.) might work differently in one form of communication (face-to-face, phone, letter, E-mail, etc.) than another. . . . On the macrolevel, medium literacy entails understanding how the widespread use of a new medium may lead to broad social changes. For example, macrolevel medium theory explores such issues as how the addition of a new medium to the matrix of existing media may alter the boundaries and nature of many social situations, reshape the relationships among people, and strengthen or weaken various social institutions. (p. 106)

This approach facilitates the comparison and contrast of various technological forms by encouraging students to consider the benefits and limits of various communication technologies. Meyrowitz realizes the potential of this method in analyzing emerging information technologies, such as the Internet, as it allows students to question "whether the increasing use of the internet, with its many alternative sources of information, including historical facts that are routinely excluded from the explanatory stories in the mainstream news media, will force the dominant, corporate news media to alter their reporting practices in order to maintain credibility with the public" (p. 106).

In addition to these three "multi-literacy" curricular models, it is vital to add a fourth component to address how all of the aforementioned "multi-literacies" are directly affected by the political and economic institutional forces of the media. Although Meyrowitz goes beyond a purely "text-centered" approach by addressing the importance of being aware of the cultural, institutional, and commercial forces that tend to lead to certain types of messages being constructed while others are avoided, this kind of analysis is rendered through an examination of media "content." Institutional analysis needs to be carried into *all* literacy so that the grammar and specific traits of the media are analyzed according to their political and economic determinations. Thus, in addition to examining how advertising and corporate funding impact the representation of nondominant groups and individuals, institutional analysis would address how visual modes of meaning and technological forms are affected by institutionalized codes and conventions, commercial funding and profit motives, media mergers, conglomerations, and global market economies—all of which delimit a plurality of voices and/ or cultural forms of expression. This kind of analysis goes hand in hand with Meyrowitz's medium theory, which explores how new technological developments affect the dominant, corporate practices of mass media (e.g., how accessing alternative information via the Internet affects mainstream news).

All of these "multi-literacy" curricular models are vital to conceptualizations of learning with and about new informational technologies, as they demand a comprehensive understanding of the specific workings of technological content, grammar, forms, and institutions in creating meaning. Taken individually, each of these media literacy methods offers important, basic skills necessary to effectively comprehend, process, and interact with the media. But if they are not all part of the learning methodology, there is the risk that key elements of media literacy will be overshadowed by others, or ignored altogether. If media *content* literacy is the sole theoretical underpinning of media education, then the elements of media *grammar* literacy essential for the deconstruction and (re)production of media alternative content are stifled. This results from a lack of understanding about how production variables specific to a medium can be manipulated to achieve a desired meaning or communication message. This poses certain difficulties for the teacher using technology. If students are strictly taught to deconstruct Web sites based on the content of a given message, they might not realize that there are commercial factors, as well as multiple design elements, affecting both the denotative and connotative interpretations of the specific message. Flashing text, the use of bold colors, interesting graphics, the size of an image, or music necessarily impact the content and purpose of messages acquired through the World Wide Web, even if they are incommensurate with the essential narrative or expository tone of the written text.

Likewise, if students are only taught skills in understanding media grammar, then their critical thinking skills would be deficient in the area of media content, as they would not necessarily learn to address "the ideas, themes, topics, information, values, ideologies, persuasive appeals, or privileged narratives of a given medium" (Meyrowitz, 1998, p. 97). Students without such proficiencies might forgo asking questions about media content elements relating to the emerging stereotypes and representations of content elements, the motivations of message producers, and the influence of media industry structures, such as the economic and political influences affecting content, or the types of messages that rarely appear in mainstream media (p. 97).

While most debates concerning media literacy are usually drawn along these two lines—namely media content literacy (theory) and media grammar literacy (production)—medium analysis must also inform media literacy, as it allows students to determine how a given medium changes the form of communication from one medium to another or from face-to-face interaction (Meyrowitz, 1998, p. 104). For example, Meyrowitz explains the importance of learning to compare and contrast media forms by examining (a) the type of sensory information conveyed (visual, oral, olfactory, etc.); (b) the form of information within each sense (picture versus written word); (c) the degree of definition, resolution, fidelity (a radio voice is closer to a live voice than a television close-up is to a real face); (d) the unidirectional, bidirectional, or multidirectional capacity of communication; (e) the speed and degree of immediacy in encoding, dissemination, and decoding; (f) the relative ease or difficulty of learning to produce and deconstruct media along various stages of mastery (learning to read versus learning to listen to the radio); and so forth. Through this kind of analysis, students are better able to distinguish and recognize how media environments change according to the communication form. This also enables students to explore how the widespread use of a new medium leads to broad social change (p. 105). This is especially important in the area of new information technologies, such as the Internet, as it allows students to look at how communication and networking between groups and individuals are affected by electronically transmitted communication, and allows students to discover alternate sources of information otherwise absent in mainstream media.

Finally, the institutional analysis of the media must inform discussions surrounding media content and grammar, as both are ultimately determined by political and economic forces. Without this understanding, students would not see the necessary interconnections between values, ideologies, persuasive appeals, privileged narratives and ownership, conglomerate power, commercialization, materialism, and consumerism. At the essence of any critical "medium theory" is an analysis of how commercial forces impede upon the potential for broad social changes to emerge from new information technologies.

Pedagogically, each of the four modes of literacy entertains different classroom possibilities. Media content literacy affords students the chance to develop their analytical skills by questioning and problematizing the content of various messages. This is vital in the area of technology, as it allows students to go beyond the acquisition of computer-mediated content by providing them with the mechanisms necessary to critically analyze and interrogate the presumed meanings within a given text. Using a political economic framework, students can discover how content is directly related to media ownership, profit, deregulation, and manipulation. Such skills are elemental to fostering critical autonomy. Media grammar literacy enables students to comprehend as well as maneuver the variables that constitute message content. If students are expected to "talk-back" *to* the media *through* the media, they must be able to understand and selectively manipulate the grammar and institutional variables of a given medium by learning empowerment skills in media production. And medium literacy offers students more knowledgeable choices about the various modes of communication and their impact than those choices traditionally permitted in the classroom. Thus students can compare the amount of information available in a newspaper article with that available in broadcast-news soundbites. This enables them to decide which communication medium best represents a message and which does not. Production skills associated with medium theory and institutional analysis also permit students to decide which media forms and distribution outlets best suit their needs. For those whose competencies or learning strengths are best communicated through written media, they can opt to deliver their point of view through Web-page publishing, word-processing, or e-mail; students who are proficient in visual media can choose to attain a level of achievement through video, television, or multimedia production.

Naturally, the careful balance of all four modes of media literacy leads to the most effective form of critical learning. The model of multiple media literacies conceptualized by Meyrowitz (1998) suggests that "there is no finite set of knowledge that will make someone media literate, and that it is unrealistic to expect any given media literacy program to teach all that we could hope children and adults would know about media" (p. 108). Notwithstanding, these aspects of media literacy will be helpful in thinking about effective approaches aimed at teaching students to be media literate in cyberspace.

## DRIVER EDUCATION FOR CYBERSPACE: DEVELOPING LITERACY SKILLS IN MEDIA CONTENT, MEDIA GRAMMAR, AND MEDIUM THEORY

In documenting the obstacles to the development of media education in the United States, Robert Kubey (1998) contends that there is a lack of support from parents, as well as from teachers and administrators, who want their children to be computer literate rather than media literate. As Kubey explains, "parents believe that computer expertise can equal a leg up in the job market" (p. 60). While workplace concerns have long dominated U.S. education, the merging of computer, information, and media literacy skills is long overdue. With the proliferation of computer-mediated information technologies in schools, students are faced with the challenge of learning not only how to acquire useful information through new technologies, but more importantly, how to critically analyze and evaluate information once it's been retrieved and deciphered. This critical learning process is only becoming more arduous with the proliferation of information forms and sources. In *Critical Thinking* (1998), Richard Paul opines:

> The fundamental characteristic of the world students now enter is ever-accelerating change; a world in which information is multiplying even as it is swiftly becoming obsolete and out of date, a world in which ideas are continually restructured, retested, and rethought. (cited in Quesada & Lockwood Summers, 1998, p. 30)

Consequently, one of the basic tenets of a cyber-based media literacy resulting from information overload is learning how to carefully and intelligently navigate your way through the Internet. As Arli Quesada and Sue Lockwood Summers (1998) explain, "if we expect today's students to be able to construct knowledge applicable to their daily lives—which are filled with information coming at them in various forms of media—teachers need to learn how to use media to their advantage" (p. 30). For many teachers who are new to the Internet, this means overcoming anxiety about "safety" concerns impeding critical, student-directed learning. Furthermore, some media education approaches cultivate anxiety and despair among students through approaches that teach students facts and examples of how the media manipulate us, how we are cultural dupes, and how we are always already trapped by ideology. This pedagogical strategy continues to perpetuate a "protec-tionist" stance among teachers. Such an approach assumes that students are always already-duped by cultural ideology—that the omnipotent media will continually entrap and disenable students from transforming meaning (Buckingham, 1992). In order to foster independent learning that goes beyond the classroom walls, teachers need to acknowledge that their positions as "radical" educators or "teachers-as-critics" will not always be accepted by students. Teachers must expect more from their students than their acquiescing to the teacher's "radical" or "liberal" point of view. Through responsible Internet use, teachers need to devise practical and pedagogically effective ways to make the Internet an engaging and enriching learning tool in the classroom and in the daily lives of students.

Using the three multiple literacies previously outlined—media content literacy, media grammar literacy, and medium literacy, as well as institutional analysis—teachers can "help students become critical consumers of information through an experiential learning process that teaches both 'about' and 'through' media" (Quesada & Lockwood Summers, 1998, p. 30). This requires pedagogical teaching methods that encourage group dialogue through the use of questioning strategies aimed at encouraging the higher levels of cognitive learning outlined in Bloom's taxonomy (1956). In order for critical autonomy to be attained, students must be motivated to learn for the sake of personal empowerment (over marketable skills) through media analysis, reflection, synthesis, and evaluation. The next section of this chapter provides some illustrative examples of how media literacy can work in schools and classrooms using the Internet.

### Media Content Literacy

One of the most important conceptions of Internet access involves not only how much information we can acquire, but also the quality of the information we receive. When using the Internet, three essential questions need to be asked in order to evaluate what we stand to gain by this new technology: (1) How well can we make discerning judgments about what we read? (2) What ideas and issues are available on the Internet? and (3) What absences and silences exist, or what is not to be found there?

Due to the vast array of information present on the Internet and its importance as a communication and research resource for all areas of study, use and exploration of this medium is commonplace at most schools and universities, and it is becoming an important part of college prep instruction. Unfortunately, just as there is accurate and important information accessible over the Internet, there is also much that is inappropriate for academic purposes. This is especially troubling for teachers. Educator David Crossman (1997) explains:

> Many teachers whose students use the Web are concerned about the question of authenticity and reliability of information on the Internet in general and the Web in particular. Even the most casual evening of Web surfing reveals incredible amounts of trivia, misinformation, bad manners, hostility, stupidity, and other vagaries of humankind. (p. 32)

Using Meyrowitz's media-as-conduits metaphor, Internet content literacy carefully considers the value and reliability of information acquired through the World Wide Web. While few education models apply content literacy to the Internet, library media specialists are on the forefront of devising content literacy skills enabling students to question the veracity of the information they receive online. Drawing from the "College Library" online resource at the University of California, Los Angeles, there are many analytical questions to be asked when thinking critically about discipline-based World Wide Web resources. The majority of these questions are centered around content and evaluation.

One of the first evaluative questions for Web resources investigates the information provider or source. By asking who is the originator, creator, or author of a Web site (or e-mail), students can determine if a Web site claims to represent a group, an organization, an institution, a corporation, or a governmental body. At the root of this question are concerns regarding the reliability and representativeness of the information acquired. Teachers would want their students to look at the Web address provided on the home or front page of the site in order to get clues as to whether the information comes from a university or trustworthy institution, or whether it is from an anonymous individual whose credibility would need verification. It would be advisable for students to verify the qualifications of content authors, sponsors, or supporters. Students would want to find out if the Web site is officially or unofficially endorsed or sponsored by particular groups, organizations, institutions, and the like, as this again impacts the credibility of the information acquired.

The next evaluative question aims to discover if the Web site or e-mail claims to describe or provide the results of research or scholarly effort. In terms of basic research skills, it makes sense for librarians to instill in their students a curiosity regarding whether or not there are sufficient references provided to other works, to document hypotheses, claims, or assertions. By asking if there is enough information to properly cite the document, students can decide if the information they've found is appropriate for a research report. Students would want to know if the Web site/e-mail combines educational, research, and scholarly information with commercial or noncommercial product or service marketing, as this affects the underlying goals or objectives of the site. Accordingly, the purpose of a Web site should be clearly indicated. One means of enabling students to determine the motivations of the Web content providers is to click on the privacy policy, which is usually located at the bottom of a Web page in small font size.

By inquiring into the economic or political influences of Internet content, students should question whether the ratio of useful information to superfluous information is adequate. They would want to pay attention to the amount of advertising, as well as to unrelated graphics or links, as these factors necessarily impact the content. For instance, if information on oral hygiene is provided by the manufacturer of a toothpaste seeking to influence brand-name loyalty, students should be more skeptical of the claims being made within the site. Other profit motives include fees for the use of access to any of the information provided at a site. Naturally, students would want to determine whether such fees are warranted or whether similar information could be found for free on other sites, or through other research tools. In terms of politics, students would want to discover the motives, values, and ideas influencing the content so that they could better sort through and evaluate the claims and assertions projected on a Web site.

Finally, the timeliness of online information would need to be fathomed so that students could discern whether or not the study or research on the Web site/e-mail is up-to-date. If the date of the information is not easily located within the content, students could look for the last update to the page or site at the bottom of the front or home page. This enables students to judge the accuracy of the information garnered based on recent scholarship, discoveries, or perspectives that affect previous findings.

As Meyrowitz (1998) explains, content literacy skills are not exclusive to any media per se, but are easily applicable from one medium to another. Students can employ these same evaluative questions in studying books, newspapers, magazines, television programs, and other texts. Certainly, there are some unconventional circumstances presented by Internet content that set the Internet apart from other research tools. There are vast amounts of information available on any given topic, allowing students more flexibility in conducting research than a school library might offer. Nevertheless, students must first figure out how to find the type of information they are looking for, which requires skills in conducting effective online excursions using various search engines. While students can always go to a librarian or teacher for search tips or strategies, it is not always easy to figure out which

Internet sites are worthy of perusal and which ones should be avoided. Consequently, teachers must equip students with the right set of critical content literacy skills so that they are prepared to access, analyze, and evaluate online messages. Librarians and teachers will still need to offer students online resource sites that help students find other educational sites relevant to research. Pedagogically, teachers will need to devise methods of allowing students to experiment and engage with Internet technology through activities that encourage them to sharpen and apply their critical thinking strategies to this particular technology.

## Media Grammar Literacy

While there is nothing prodigious in applying critical evaluative questions to the Internet, the critical study and utilization of the Internet is distinctive in terms of its media grammar and form. For this reason, media literacy in cyberspace must go beyond online content literacy by addressing the peculiarities of the Internet as a communication technology. As mentioned earlier, media grammar literacy for the Internet requires an understanding of the production elements used to alter people's understanding of messages communicated electronically. As such, teachers would want their students to learn graphic design principles so that they better understand how Web pages are created or infused with carefully crafted signifiers. Vibrant colors, large fonts, flashing text, striking visuals, and music used to draw or divert attention need to be decoded so that students ascertain the function, intention, or goal served by the graphics, icons, and design elements.

Subsequently, the basic elements of graphic design usually reserved for art or vocational curricula need to be integrated across the curriculum so that students can better comprehend how various production elements work to signify or connote particular meanings in cyberspace. Since the Internet is necessarily nonlinear in form, there are many design elements used to feature certain areas, visuals, or links. Whether these elements are used for business, educational, or civic means, students would want to evaluate the creativity and effectiveness involved in the structural design of the message by asking: (a) What media elements are used to communicate? (e.g., words, pictures, sounds, videos, animations, etc.), and (b) How is the content organized? (e.g., through user-controlled hypertext or hypermedia links).

As a component of media grammar literacy, visual literacy theory has been used to encourage students to produce and interpret visual messages. In *Visual Messages* (1992), David Considine and Gail Haley explain that, like traditional literacy, visual literacy embraces what might be termed a "reading and writing component" (p. 15). Students can be taught to recognize, read, recall, and comprehend visual messages. Accordingly, students who understand the design and composition of visual messages can better achieve communication through visual means. With the rapid increase in student-designed Web pages, design elements converged around Internet technology are becoming more necessary. By using the components of visual literacy that have been applied to audio, moving images, and still graphics, students can better think *about* and *through* the images and multisensory components of the Internet.

### Medium Literacy

Media grammar literacy, or visual literacy, includes an understanding of the medium and the message, the form as well as the content. In terms of the Internet, medium analysis would require students to examine the variables previously described in Meyrowitz's multiple-literacies model. In particular, Internet technology impacts (a) the multisensory types of information conveyed, as the Internet communicates messages through visual, aural, and textual means; (b) the uni/bi/multidirectionality of the communication, which is affected by Internet postings, e-mail correspondence between individuals, and chat-room discussions between two or more people; and (c) the speed and degree of immediacy in encoding, dissemination, and decoding, which are altered by the Internet's instantaneous message transmission and its ability to bring otherwise disjointed individuals or groups together in non–face-to-face encounters. These are among some of the variables students would need to analyze when using the Internet.

One of most critical applications of medium theory would lead students to examine how message variables, both content and visual, are uniquely acquired and represented in cyberspace. Students must learn to question whether the information they find is unique to the Internet or is available through print and other non-Internet resources. This inquiry leads students to understand the potential of the Internet as a decentralized form of technology, since it greatly increases the amount of information and perspectives (both dominant and nondominant) available on any given topic. This presents creative opportunities for students to find ideas and messages that rarely unfold in mainstream media. Moreover, through user-controlled hypertext or hypermedia links, students can "interactively" determine what informational course they want to navigate. Unlike mass communication technologies controlled by gatekeepers and conventions, students will have more freedom in determining for themselves what sources they wish to retrieve information from online. Moreover, students need to compare and contrast the uniqueness of online communication, as nonverbal cues, voice inflection, and even inferences usually deducted through face-to-face correspondence are usually absent from the Internet (or delayed with the use of Web-cams). Educational prospects such as these can only unfold in the critical thinking classroom, whereby students are encouraged to discover, compare and contrast, and critique the messages communicated through computer information technology.

## PUTTING THEORY INTO PRACTICE: DESIGNING CYBER-LITERACY LESSONS

In order for students to become cyber-literate, teachers must design and employ critical learning lessons that go beyond merely using technology for its own sake. Few resources have been devised to help students understand the constructed nature of Internet communication. As Quesada and Lockwood Summers (1998) explain, students need to realize that

> information presented in various print and electronic sources can have commercial, ideological, and political implications. This is critical awareness in American society where major television and publishing networks are controlled by a handful of corporations and more than half of the sites on the Internet are commercial. Of the Web sites created for other than commercial purposes, many have their own agendas that motivate their designers to spread the word electronically.

In response to these concerns, Quesada and Lockwood Summers offer some important suggestions and strategies in critically engaging students with Internet technology. First, students need to understand that all media are symbolic sign systems that re-present (not reflect) reality (Masterman, 1989, cited in Quesada & Lockwood Summers, 1998). In order to better comprehend this concept, students can brainstorm the multiple sources of information by categorizing, reflecting upon, and discussing both form (the format, such as television) and content (the actual text, images, sounds, and substance of the message). By separating the variables of print and electronic sources, students can more readily understand how form and content are related in each medium. Once students have created a list of information sources, teachers should ask questions that help them deconstruct the production elements, or media grammar, used to create meaning. They would want to consider what media variables (words, pictures, sounds, video, animation, etc.) are used to communicate the message, and how the content is organized (linear or nonlinear, mass communicated or decentralized, interactive or noninteractive). Through small- and large-

group discussions, students would want to discuss which media elements (words, pictures, animations, special effects, etc.) or combination
of elements have the most impact, and why.

After expressing their media viewpoints and the experiences that
impact their feelings and emotive responses, teachers would want to
address medium literacy by having students think about the benefits
and drawbacks of different forms of print and electronic communication. Quesada and Lockwood Summers (1998) offer a useful lesson
whereby students match the content of various informational sources
to practical research situations. If they are looking for up-to-the-minute
data, students should be asked if they are more likely to find it in a
daily newspaper, in a monthly magazine, or on the World Wide Web.
If they want a historical view, are they more likely to find it in a book,
print encyclopedia, CD-ROM reference tool, video documentary, or on
Web TV? Which sources provide local data? Which ones are more international in scope?

Taking Quesada and Lockwood Summers's lesson one step further,
it would be important for students to consider which sources go beyond
the mainstream, providing them with nondominant, alternative information that challenges the ideological, political, and economic motivations of data sources. Because students aren't always aware of
nonmainstream alternatives, teachers would want to provide students
with multimedia resources allowing them to critically question and
(re)engage with those sources they most frequently encounter. This
leads to many useful lessons designed to encourage students to analyze
and evaluate the significance and credibility of media forms. Students
should be encouraged to go back to their comprehensive list of information sources in order to identify which resources (the nightly news,
for example) contain information that is "prefiltered" by experts, authorities, sponsors, and advertisers, and which ones are "unfiltered"
(Internet chat rooms). Teachers would want their students to consider
the validity of sources such as infomercials in which "experts" endorse
a particular product (Quesada & Lockwood Summers, 1998).

After students conduct research in which they select a controversial
issue and bring in examples of prefiltered and unfiltered information
from various media sources—magazines, newspapers, videos, CD-
ROMs, Web sites—to compare and discuss, teachers should ask students about the resources found in their research. Quesada and
Lockwood Summers (1998) offer the following sample questions:

- Whose point of view is being expressed?
- Is the author a noted expert in the field or a researcher who has
  acknowledged credibility?

- Is the information fact or opinion—or a mixture of both?
- Are examples or evidence given to support statements or conclusions made?
- Is there a built-in bias due to political, economic, or social agenda?
- Who is the intended audience?
- Are the vocabulary, tone, illustrations, and other media elements appropriate for the intended audience?
- Is the data current or no longer valid?
- Are there inconsistencies in the information presented?
- What's not being told and why?
- Can you identify any persuasive techniques being used?

Teachers should encourage students to talk about these points and follow up with student-directed activities. For example, students could be asked to identify specific statements of fact and opinion or persuasive techniques within their media examples; they could then represent these examples offering a different viewpoint, changing the intended audience, manipulating the graphics, and so forth, in order to see how the manipulation of media variables alters the information and its decoding (Quesada & Lockwood Summers, 1998).

While the previous questions are applicable to most media forms, there are activities that are specific to the Internet. Based on activities from MEDIA ALERT! 200 Activities to Create Media-Savvy Kids, there are six steps that students can use in judging Web sites. First, students should not be fooled by appearance. Although the design elements of a Web site might look more professional, intriguing, or appealing than the design elements of other media, the information contained within a Web site might be inaccurate and unreliable. A visually flamboyant site with multisensory capabilities like music, video, and animation might be a facade for marketing ploys aimed at encouraging brand loyalty or product consumption, or propaganda aimed at influencing attitudes and behavior.

Second, teachers need to help students locate guides they can trust. Resource lists, "hotlists," and other authorities suggested by teachers or students that can be trusted to offer valuable educational sites should be bookmarked. With the help of teachers and librarians, students can find many reputable resource indexes and clearinghouses that rate sites according to a variety of subject areas.

Third, students need to discover who's behind the information. Students should check if the author or creator is listed, or if there are links to a page listing the professional credentials or affiliations of the author or creator. If no authorship, group, or institution is listed, then students should be extremely skeptical of the information provided. If they are looking at a message in a Usenet newsgroup or Internet mailing list, they should check if the author has included a "signature"—a short, often biographical description that's automatically appended to the end of messages. Many people include their credentials in their signature or point to their home page, where they provide biographical information.

Fourth, students need to find out why the information was posted. Web sites are published by for-profit business, nonprofit organizations, professional and trade organizations, government agencies, educational institutions, individual researchers, political and advocacy groups, and hobbyists, and each constituent has its own agenda, whether it is explicitly stated or hidden. Students must learn to detect the agenda when visiting these sites, or when participating in online discussions.

The fifth Internet guideline is to look for the date the information was created or modified. Unless students are conducting historical research, current information is generally more valid and useful than older material. If the Web site doesn't contain a "last updated" indicator or date its content, students should carefully examine its links. If more than a few links are no longer working, the information is likely to be out-of-date.

Finally, students should get in the habit of verifying the same information elsewhere. If students find vastly contradictory information or outlandish claims running counter to common sense, it would be wise for them to check other sources of information. Ideally, students should check the information with two or more additional sources.

While such referential questions and guidelines are inevitably useful and beneficial for students conducting online research, they tend to send up red flags about the hazards of receiving information via Internet transmission. Unfortunately, the critical questions previously explained do not necessarily equip students with visions as to how the Internet can be used to provide useful information otherwise absent from mediated sources. Due to its decentralization, a vast array of perspectives, opinions, and research can be obtained on the Internet with the proper search skills. While students clearly benefit from asking critically loaded questions about Internet content, they should also feel competent about acquiring the type of information most beneficial to their research or knowledge base.

For many, the Internet has been influential in supplying otherwise unavailable data or knowledge in limited circulation. In the medical field, the Internet has been especially useful in connecting doctors, patients, and concerned family members within and across nations in efforts to ascertain and share medical treatments, options, or alternatives to diagnoses and illnesses. Concerned groups and citizens examining political and economic issues or controversies can find subcultural cyber-groups aiming to provide different narratives or explanations of events, perspectives, and historical documentation. For consumers, the Internet has been influential in helping people discover the wholesale prices of automobiles, appliances, and furniture, as well as the best mortgage rates, real estate prices, and other consumable goods. Moreover, people can participate and interact more freely in cyberspace through Internet postings, cyber–chat rooms, e-mail, and Web-page design than in top-down, linear, mass modes of communication, such as television and print communication. In these capacities, the equation of "who knows what about whom through what media" is altered so that the public is theoretically able to access the same information as private corporations or institutions. Of course, proficiencies in computer skills and access to computer terminals affect access. But as Internet access continues to rapidly grow in schools, students need to go beyond cyber-savvy skepticism by learning to make use of the creative and informed possibilities provided by Internet technology.

### Cyber-Literacy Lesson 1

Using the techniques offered by Quesada and Lockwood Summers (1998), and MEDIA ALERT!, I've devised a set of lessons specific to the acquisition and critical evaluation of information from the World Wide Web that can be adapted and employed in the classroom. Although the following lesson sample was designed for teachers concerned about gender equity, the general thrust of this learning exploration is easily applicable to other subject areas, foci, and special topics. The crux of the lesson entails the comparison and contrast of two online cyber-magazines that represent different objectives and information sources. For the purpose of this exercise, the sites chosen delineate prospective areas of interest to teenage girls in middle and high school grade levels. In the classroom, teachers employing this learning exercise should encourage students to select their own comparative Web sites that interest them, as this creates personal investment in the subject of study.

The first Web site for this lesson is the cyber-version of *Seventeen* magazine (www.seventeen.com). Like its print version, *Seventeen Online* provides teenage girls with fashion and beauty tips, horoscopes, entertainment information, and advice on love and sex. The front or home page is the first place where teachers would want their students to begin their critical exploration of the site. By asking, "What do you see?" students should be encouraged to write a list detailing the denotative, or plainly observable, aspects of the page they examine. In this case, students would observe singer/songwriter Jewel on the cover of *Seventeen* magazine with her shoulders exposed and draped in a garment. They would remark on the graphics displaying one girl sipping coffee and another listening to a Walkman. Toward the bottom of the page, there is a section titled "Entertainment Buzz," which has a picture displaying actor Michael Vartan. Finally, there are columns of text highlighting magazine stories, contests, events, voting ballots, and the like.

Once a class list of observations is generated from each individual, teachers need to have students analyze and evaluate what they see. This step encourages students to think about the connotative, or interpretive, aspects of the ad by making sense of the codes used to signify meaning. Since the process of seeing is inherently personal and subjective, students should work individually in recording their interpretations so that they examine what the various details of the page mean to them. Through a small- and large-group discussion, students can talk about how they each made their own meaning from the images in the advertisement (decoding).

In order to pay attention to the intended meaning or "production values" (encoding), teachers should work with students to generate a list of techniques used in making the Web site. In terms of these criteria, students should comment on the use of color, font size, graphics, and photographs used to make some aspects of the page stand out over others. By looking at the pictures provided, they might observe specific beauty standards set within the photos (e.g., making the girls look older through dress and makeup), the passivity of "girl-specific" activities (sipping coffee and listening to a Walkman), and the amount of entertainment trivia aimed to direct action through consumption (e.g., "Alanis and Tori will be channeling stadiums full of female rage in a town near you! We'll help you hop aboard this caravan of catharsis.").

More sophisticated analyses would incorporate an evaluation of the motives or goals influencing the content and design of *Seventeen*'s Web site. By looking at where the links to the page are located, students would discover that the "interactive" features are limited to participation in entertainment trivia voting polls ("*Vote Now* for the Teen Choice Awards!"), *Seventeen*-sponsored events and contests ("Win a $500 Shopping Spree!"), and horoscope readings intertwining love advice with popular television and film stars ("*Leo*, will you click like Monica and Chandler or have a Ross and Rachel rift? Find out as we peruse the planetary positions.")

Through synergy, the "cyber-interactions" within *Seventeen*'s Web site are used to make reference to and market products consumable by the intended target audience. Students can more directly make sense of these profit-making motives by examining the privacy policy, contest rules, and Web-site provider located at the bottom of the page. Naturally, the critical student will take note of the placement and conspicuously small type of these links. By reviewing *Seventeen*'s online privacy policy, students can quite easily uncover the goals or objectives of the Web site. Although the cyber-magazine claims to value and preserve the privacy of its visitors and registered users, the charmingly witty vernacular offered within the policy link tells another story:

> What's Elvis got to do with it? Basically Seventeen Online uses the information we gather about you to custom fit our site according to your likes and dislikes, as well as those of our advertisers. Say we write a quiz about Elvis, you know, the King of Rock 'n Roll and we see that thousands of you took to and enjoyed the quiz. Well, that means that we're sure to run a "Do You Love Me Tender?" quiz in honor of Elvis the next chance we get. Why? Because you told us you were into Elvis. We might also use this same Elvis info to help the folks in marketing develop a line of fat-free Elvis cookies. And then perhaps one of our advertisers might call Seventeen Online and ask how many people "clicked" on the ad they ran next to that wacky Elvis quiz. See? We get all that useful information from one click of your mouse. . . . We might also send out emails to users that have opted for an online service to announce special offers, services and announcements from our site and/or our advertisers. (1999, p. 2)

Students should also be encouraged to find out about the Web-site provider. By clicking on "PRIMEDIA," the publisher for *Seventeen* magazine, links connected to the publisher's related online publications—SoapDigest.com, ChannelOne.com, and UltimateGiftGuide.com—can be acquired. By looking at PRIMEDIA's related business affiliates, the interconnections between information, entertainment, advertising, and marketing are easily detectable. Once such marketing ploys are unveiled, students can better understand how the means of "self-expression," "free choice," and "participation" are delineated within a profit-driven cyber-system of consumption. The goal of this process is not to have students interpret the motives of the Web-site provider as inherently good or bad as the teacher might see it, but to allow students to "see outside the box," or as Judith Williamson (1992) puts it, see ideology on their own terms, thus enabling them to make everyday choices with this contextual knowledge in mind.

In addition to locating the denotative, connotative, and motivational elements of the site, teachers need to ask students, "What's missing?" so that students learn to juxtapose the stories, experiences, and visual representations of the Web site with their lives and environments. In terms of the experiences represented with *Seventeen*'s Web site, the menu link titled "Trauma-rama" packages concerns faced by teenage girls by publishing amusing tales and anecdotes about mildly unpleasant or embarrassing moments, usually pertaining to shopping, fashion, and meeting boys:

thumbs-down

My friend and I live in a fairly small town where there are only a few good shops. One day, as we strolled from store to store, my friend dared me to stick out my thumb like I was hitchhiking. Being the daredevil that I am, I did it, and was surprised when a car actually stopped. But I was unlucky—the person who pulled up was my mom! I haven't seen daylight since.

nowhere to hide

Without asking my older sister first, I borrowed her pants and then said I didn't know where they were. Too bad for me, I was wearing them the day my sister came to my school to play in a basketball game. When she saw me, she was really steamed. She threatened to rip the pants off me, so I ran away from her. When I got home, our parents grounded me good.

lying like a rug

My parents say I'm not allowed to date until next year, but I really wanted to go to the movies with this guy. I told my mom that he was my friend's cousin and that his mom was taking us all to the movies. When he came over by himself to pick me up, I said we were going back to get his mom and my friend, who was still blow-drying her hair. My mom said she would catch me if I was lying. After we left, my mom called to see if his mother had taken us to the movies, which, of course, she hadn't. I couldn't leave the house for a month! (1999, compiled by Holly Charron)

By looking at other teen-directed Web sites, students can begin the second part of the lesson, which is to contrast the content and form of two or more cyber-magazines. A good alternative site designed for this unit on gender equity is *Teen Voices Online* (www.teenvoices.com). Self-described as a cyber-magazine "about girls being themselves and realizing their potential," the denotative and connotative elements of this site stand in stark contrast to *Seventeen Online*. Once again, the teacher would begin by asking students to articulate what they see on the home or front page. In this case, there is one photograph displaying the current cover issue of the print magazine version at the top of the page. On this cover, there are three smiling teenage girls: one African

American, one Asian, and one Latino. Contrary to the sexualized, air-brushed cover photo of music artist Jewel (who is not a teenager), the three nonwhite girls portrayed in *Teen Voices* look their age and are wearing everyday attire. The text/moto beneath the visual states: "because you're more than just a pretty face."

Unlike the flashy images and text within *Seventeen Online*, the front page of *Teen Voices* is fairly simple, with only four menu links—"Get Involved," "About Teen Voices," "Get Teen Voices," and "Contact Us." In moving toward connotative interpretation, students can state what they believe the images and layout on the page represent. Observations should make mention of the connotations raised by the girls' racial diversity, facial expressions, clothing, and proximity. In terms of layout, students could make inferences about the lack of sophisticated graphics, text links, and other grammar variables (e.g., small budget resulting from little to no advertising).

By clicking onto "About Teen Voices" and examining the content of the stories featured in the issue, students can discover the primary goals or objectives of the cyber-zine. The mission statement reads:

> Teen Voices is more than just a magazine because we believe that you are more than just a pretty face. Teen Voices is about girls being themselves and realizing their potential. There are enough magazines that tell girls how to look and act to impress a boy or buy certain products. Teen Voices honors the authentic voices of teenage and young adult women. Teen Voices challenges the mainstream media's image of girls by providing an intelligent alternative packed with original writing, poetry and artwork. We encourage our readers to write articles on self-esteem, racism, sexism, feminism, popular culture, health, and other issues important to them. (2000)

Unlike *Seventeen Online*'s trivialization of issues affecting teenage girls, the stories featured in *Teen Voices Online* deal with hard-hitting issues and circumstances experienced and written by/for other teenagers. The titles of the stories provide a glimpse of the subjects covered within the issue categories: "Coping with the Loss of a Friend to Suicide," "Teen Motherhood—What You Can Do If You Become Pregnant," "Surviving Sexual Assault and Dealing with Date Rape," "Health—Eating Your Way to Easier PMS," "The Maori and Kiwis Living in New Zealand," "Surviving and Thriving with Juvenile Arthritis," "Music Reviews—Cadallaca and Tori Amos," "Career Choices after High School: Interviews with Young Women." These subjects can be contrasted with *Seventeen Online*'s article categories: "Daily Cafe (New Romances among Stars)," "Horoscopes," "Trauma-rama," "Entertainment Buzz,"

"Love & Sex," "Style File," "Contests & Quizzes," "Deal with It," and "What You Say."

What's more, while interactive participation in *Seventeen Online* is reserved for consumption and marketing, *Teen Voices* encourages the submissions of articles, poems, artwork, or reviews by teens. There is even a call for young adults interested in working for the magazine: "openings are available for academic unpaid internships, workstudy students, and volunteers age 18 or older." This information is critical in helping students find out the demographics (age group, gender, etc.) as well as the philosophy and motivations of the contributing writers and publishers of *Teen Voices*. Such information helps students appraise the level of similarities and differences between themselves and the contributing authors/publishers.

When drawing conclusions about advertising and subscription solicitation within each online Web site, students should compare the varying degrees and tactics employed to sell products. For many reasons, *Teen Voices Online* is incomparable with *Seventeen Online* in terms of its discreetness (ads are contained within a few designated links), ethics (it only sells approved products that are commensurate with the magazine's philosophy of promoting self-esteem among girls), and volume (it does not contain nearly as many ads as *Seventeen*). Obviously, the financial underpinnings of the cyber-magazines impact the effectiveness of the techniques used in persuading students to subscribe to the print version of the magazine, as well as the products featured within the online magazine. Students should discuss which of the two sites contains compelling ads and which does not. This discussion should also carry over into a discussion of how personal preference, response, and pleasure are derived from each site. One of the best approaches to teaching students to acknowledge their complicitness within mass culture/popular culture is for teachers to acknowledge their own complicated relationship with the media as teachers, citizens, consumers, parents, and the like. In her book *Where the Girls Are* (1994), Susan Douglas makes the important point that teachers and cultural workers need to acknowledge the pleasures, pains, and contradictions experienced in media viewing. Naturally, this process is applicable to Internet use for both entertaining as well as informative means.

In this lesson, cyber-magazines provide a simple yet interesting exploration of how print media are altered when extended to electronic media. Moreover, through the exploration of alternative, nonmainstream sites such as *Teen Voices Online*, lessons on medium literacy can unfold in order to demonstrate the possibilities of finding nondominant information. Unlike grocery- and convenience-store aisles chockfull of mainstream-only publications, both *Seventeen Online* and *Teen*

*Voices Online* can be accessed with the click of a mouse. But in order for students to know about *Teen Voices Online*, they must acquire some knowledge about which "alternative" sites, links, and resources to explore. Such knowledge is complicated by the advertising of mainstream Web sites through other media forms—television commercials and print ads now rarely advertise a product without divulging their related Web site. Media mergers, like Disney's acquisition of search engine Go.com and the merger between Time Warner and AOL, will undoubtedly increase the difficulties faced by nonmainstream publications, information sources, groups, and individuals wanting to let people know they exist.[1] Consequently, the need for good, solid cyber-info search strategies goes hand in hand with the need for critical learning ventures on the Internet.

### Cyber-Literacy Lesson 2

In designing and implementing critical exercises specific to the Internet, a variety of Web sites pertaining to any subject can be employed. In my own teaching, I've designed and employed other related cyber-based lessons in order to teach students about media production elements so that students understand and evaluate their limited capacity to "speak out" through commercial media. In this activity, teachers can choose a media form that students are invested in, like television, film, or music, in order to encourage critical thinking about their degree of participation or action in mass culture/popular culture. In addition to generating interest in the lesson, the use of pop culture in the classroom serves a pedagogical function. As Judith Williamson argues in "How Does Girl Number Twenty Understand Ideology?" (1992), the best ways to help students detect "invisible" ideology is by relating ideology to those experiences that directly affect students' lives, through those contradictions that threaten their own well-being or that conflict with a change of experience (p. 83). Accordingly, the teacher would need to structure learning activities that directly involve and implicate students.

Through this particular lesson, teachers can reinforce critical "cyber-surfing" skills by comparing and contrasting RollingStone.com (www. rollingstone.com) with the Web site *Your Own MusicReviews* (www. home1.pacific.net.sg/~tengo/music.html). While *Rolling Stone* began as a semi-subcultural outlet for rock music fans, students can evaluate the online magazine by reviewing its titillating graphics, "Real Time" music video and audio clips, exclusive interviews, reviews, contests, and concert information and news coverage. As leading questions, teachers can ask, "Have you ever disagreed with a music review that's been published in *Rolling Stone* magazine or other music publications?"

**Table 6.1**
**Five Basic Questions and Concepts of Media Literacy**

| |
|---|
| 1. Who is telling the story and why? / Media construct reality |
| 2. How are they telling the story? / Media use unique languages |
| 3. What is the story they are telling? / Media have commercial interests |
| 4. How will different people understand the story? / Audiences create different meanings based on their experiences and interpretations |
| 5. What is missing? Whose story is not being told? / Media express values and points of view |

and "Have you ever wanted to contribute or publish your own review of your favorite rock, alternative, or pop group or artist?" By taking students to the Web site, the five basic questions/concepts of media literacy represented in Table 6.1 can be applied to RollingStone.com.

As in the previous exercise, individual, small-, and large-group discussions can emerge from student findings. Once students have made their own evaluations, teachers can provide additional related information in order to help students assess and evaluate the site. For example, teachers can make reference to the fact that *Rolling Stone* has gone outside the publishing world to name an advertising executive, John Berg, to lead its three magazines. Teachers would want to let students make their own inferences about how this affects content and signals a continuing push by magazine companies to form closer ties with the advertising community to increase profits.

Upon looking at the music reviews provided in RollingStone.com, most of which are upbeat and are directly linked to influencing the purchase of CDs and concert tickets, students can frequent another music-review Web site, *Your Own MusicReviews*, organized specifically as an interactive medium for people to read and solicit personal, non-commercially motivated music reviews. Despite its text-oriented style devoid of flashy music-artist photos or graphics, students will quickly notice a difference in the variety of music reviews on a number of genres and performers. Not only can people offer their own musical ratings from the site's choices (e.g., "At least the cover looks good," "Wanna buy over from me or not?" "I will definitely rob to get this,") but they can also provide lengthy expository reviews. Here are selected examples of variant opinions on performer Alanis Morissette's album *Jagged Little Pill*:

I have to say it is pretty good. I do think she could've done better. One problem is the lyrics. Why would anyone say "well isn't this nice" while they're about to die? More like "and as the plane crashed down he said 'Ahhhhhhhhh!'" And then there's the chorus. She sounds like she's destroying everything and everyone. We probably only like her because of her mental breakdowns. (reviewed by Steve).

Usually, i go by the saying "if you don't have anything good to say, don't say it at all." However, i'm feeling right now that i must speak out. I think alanis has a great potential. she has a beautiful voice. could have. i think if she stopped teasing her voice and let herself relax a bit, she would be much easier to listen to sometimes i think alanis is hyperventialting [sic] but alanis is who she is, and yeeha. I think a lot of people would probably like these songs. for 'mainstream', she's pretty outspoken. (reviewed by Sophie)

By comparatively analyzing and evaluating the two sites, teachers can conduct a lesson rich with implications for critical media literacy skills. Although not all of the reviews are discreetly written, teachers can encourage students to think about the pros and cons of each Web site in terms of its form, content, and grammar. Additional lessons on public access, profit, and industry regulation can be developed in conjunction with the rulings on the uses of Napster, an online music trading service that has been challenged by the profit-making recording industry. Although much of the media coverage surrounding the Napster case centered around copyright laws, teachers can discuss the importance of decentralized forms of technology that create a more democratic or level playing field for musical artists, who can break through the tight control of the recording and distribution industry by uploading their musical recordings at a low cost on the Internet.

### Cyber-Literacy Lesson 3

In addition to examining popular culture in the form of entertainment, the news industry is an interesting media structure worthy of critical analysis. With its long-standing credibility among viewers, television broadcast news has usurped the power of other dominant media forms, such as newspapers and radio, by attracting more users on a daily basis. Although more Americans get their news from television than from any other source, the limited space and institutional structure of the news establishment often prevents viewers from receiving the detailed, accurate, and investigative journalism they need to become active and educated citizens. Fortunately, the Internet provides a means through which different points of view from around the world can be instantaneously accessed through various noncommercial Web sites. One such Web site is provided by the Independent Media Center (IMC) (www.indymedia.org).

Organized as a mechanism designed to provide democratic models of global media access and news analysis, the IMC was formed one month prior to the World Trade Organization (WTO) talks and protests held in Seattle, Washington, in November 1999. In anticipation of the sparse media coverage that would be given to the WTO protests, over 500 media activists, videographers, journalists, and computer scientists from around the world worked with the IMC to contribute to the limited media coverage of the events in the mainstream news. Video footage acquired from Web-cams, video cameras, and satellite uplinks were streamed onto the Internet and supplied to a global audience via the World Wide Web on the newly launched IMC Web site.

Among some of the goals of the IMC in Seattle were: (a) to coordinate media coverage across forms of media from journalists around the world through print and electronic means; (b) to conduct interviews in the street to include sources that are usually absent from the mainstream news; and (c) to raise awareness and respond to the current structure of the media. Among its many successes, the IMC received over one million "hits" on its Web site during the WTO protests, more than the number of hits received on CNN's Web site. IMC branches have been growing exponentially in many countries and have covered important events, including the biotechnology talks and protests in Boston, the International Monetary Fund conference and protests in Washington, D.C., and the George W. Bush presidential inauguration and protests.

Using Table 6.1, teachers should begin a lesson on the comparison and contrast of dominant and nondominant news by having students ask which stories are continually represented in the news and which ones are not (content analysis), who gets news coverage (political economy/institutional analysis), and how audiences understand or respond to the news (audience analysis). Upon making such observations, students should be encouraged to apply media grammar analyses to compare/contrast the signs and symbols used in traditional news forms and online news. A medium analysis would include evaluative components on the key differences between the two news outlets so that students can decide which better represents issues relevant to them or provides the most relevant facts and information.

### Cyber-Literacy Lesson 4

The final lesson that will be offered in this chapter as a valuable teaching tool relates to the juxtaposition of current issues or controversies covered in the mainstream press and broadcast news with Internet information. Following the tragic explosion of TWA flight 800, I devised a lesson applicable to an analytical course in journalism to demonstrate to students how content is affected by the structural organization of each medium. By teaching students to seek out and critically engage with diverse viewpoints and alternative information, I chose an issue that had been receiving much media coverage and that students were somewhat familiar with. In this case, I decided to look at the chaos that emerged from the decentralized information available to the general public regarding the TWA flight 800 disaster. This case was groundbreaking for many reasons because the level of contradictory information presented through various Internet outlets caused the mainstream media to question their reporting and eventually dismiss allegations of U.S. naval involvement in the tragedy.

The incident began on July 17, 1996, when a Boeing 747 jetliner, TWA flight 800, was taking off from JFK airport on its way to Paris, France, with 230 people on board. Eleven minutes into the flight, after receiving clearance to initiate a climb to cruise altitude, the plane exploded without warning. Immediately after the incident, eyewitnesses interviewed on radio and television reported seeing a bright object "streaking" toward the 747. Given the consistent testimonies among so many eyewitnesses, the main theory regarding the cause of the explosion by experts, government officials, and pilots in the area was a surface-to-air missile. Although initial speculation about the perpetrators of a potential missile pointed the blame at "terrorists," later explanations implicated the U.S. Navy as being responsible for the incident. Despite such "rumors," the ensuing media coverage of the incident began to consider other explanations for the incident, such as a fuel-tank explosion and mechanical malfunctions, thereby downplaying the possibility that a U.S. missile caused the "accident."

Among the many interesting developments within the case reported by the mass media was that a group of "frenzied" Internet "conspirators" was accusing the U.S. government of covering up the crash of TWA flight 800. Former presidential aide and journalist Pierre Salinger held press conferences in which he claimed he had evidence, some of which originated from the Internet, of the U.S. government's involvement in the explosion. Although this information could have prompted serious news coverage of Salinger's findings, as well as relevant information about the incident made available through the Internet, the mass media scoffed at the story, caricaturing Salinger and Internet users as conspiracists while favorably focusing on the "expert" testimony of government officials and investigators.

Through its shallow coverage of the information and evidence available on the Internet, the mainstream media virtually ignored and discredited alternative information available on the Internet. Given the political economy of the mainstream media, this impertinence is not surprising, for it would not be in the best interest of the news establishment to give credence to a medium that challenges their coverage of events with alternative sources of information. Nevertheless, some interesting historical facts, evidence, and testimonies can be researched through the World Wide Web.

Without the limitations of soundbites, editorial decisionmaking, or corporate interests, Internet information on TWA flight 800 was not only abundant, but much of it was rich with contextual and historical evidence and research concerning the U.S. government. Additionally, much of the information about the incident posed serious questions about the investigation and offered facts that went unreported by media journalists. In one Web article on the subject from the International News Electronic Telegraph, an online news provider, several important questions about the investigative process of the FBI/White House were raised. Using evidence from documents released by the National Transportation Safety Board (NTSB), the article documents that

> an internal memo from the [NTSB], dated November 15, complains that sensitive radar tapes were given to the White House before they were provided to crash investigators. According to the document, the radar data indicated that a missile was converging on the Boeing 747 seconds before the aircraft broke up off the coast of Long Island, killing 230 people. Why on earth were these tapes given to the White House first? And why did the White House immediately try to quash speculation that a missile was involved? (Evans-Pritchard, 1997, p. 4)

Further referencing the NTSB document, the article explained that the NTSB was not allowed to take notes when it was shown witness statements prepared by the FBI, which confirmed that thirty-four people deemed "credible" said they saw a missile heading for the plane. The article also mentions the discrepancies between the FBI's preferred fuel-tank theory expressed in public and the findings from the NTSB, which disqualified the feasibility of such an explanation. Also mentioned were the private research initiatives of a retired pilot and an aviation consultant who, after observing a copy of a radar tape from the Federal Aviation Administration (FAA) showing a small object traveling toward the 747, maintained that the plane was downed by a missile. Upon acknowledging Salinger's claims that the missile was likely fired from the USS *Normandy* 185 miles away, as well as the investigation by the retired pilot, the online article begs the question: "So why has the FBI launched such a frantic and shrill campaign to discredit the organization's critics?" (Evans-Pritchard, 1997, p. 5).

In another detailed eight-page article posted on the World Wide Web, William Jasper (1997) investigated each of the probable theories under consideration by the FBI. With detailed information from many sources, Jasper briefly summarized the discrepancies within media reports. He explained:

> Although federal officials and various "experts" and unnamed sources quoted in media reports have largely discounted theories involving missiles in the TWA 800 downing, there are a number of facts, eyewitness reports, expert opinions, and documents which indicate that a missile attack should not be ruled out yet. Experts consulted by The New American point to a list of troubling elements. (p. 9)

Among them, Jasper listed the following: (1) reports from civilian and military eyewitnesses of an object or arc of light going up to the plane before the explosion; (2) radar recordings of an unidentified blip on the radar; (3) a photo that may show a missile streaking toward the airliner; (4) quoted misinformation in the national media about the "impossibility" of missile involvement because the 747 was beyond the alleged ranges of various missiles cited; (5) documents revealing that TWA flight 800 was flying through "hot" warning areas that the navy had reserved for "official use"; (6) official acknowledgment (after earlier denials) that various military aircraft and surface vessels were operating in the warning areas; (7) testimony from an American Airlines pilot six weeks after the TWA flight 800 crash that he saw a missile pass by his jetliner while in flight about 220 miles south of the crash site; and (8) a considerable number of precedents of previous downings of civilian aircraft. In its final point, Jasper provided readers with the U.S. State Department's past history, thereby offering a context through which the TWA flight 800 "accident" can be placed: "A U.S. State Department report lists 25 incidents in which commercial airliners were shot down by missiles, killing a total of more than 600 people" (p. 11).

Not only did the two aforementioned articles posted on the World Wide Web significantly challenge reports from the mainstream press, but they also provided new facts and insight into an incident that would otherwise be inaccessible to the average media viewer/reader. With a touch of the finger, various Web sites can be accessed detailing the U.S. Navy's past history, showing pictures from FAA radar tapes and outlining discrepancies within the media's and the government's handling of the TWA flight 800 tragedy. What's more, in addition to the availability of alternative news information and perspectives, there are several Internet discussion groups that provide citizens with the means through which to "produce" their own sites and spaces where *they* can address the TWA flight 800 incident/investigation through their personal thoughts, reactions, and skepticism. Thus, while the mainstream media decide for us what we should hear and how to make sense of things, the Web/Internet allows us to come up with our own conclusions through alternative resources and discussion groups.

Overall, the TWA flight 800 incident was abundant with critical learning elements. Upon reviewing the contradictory information presented through both mainstream and alternative media sources, students gave mixed responses. On the one hand, they were skeptical of the Internet sources they frequented, since they were not necessarily "authoritative." On the other hand, students questioned the allegiances of the mainstream press to "high-level" government sources. Even if no strong conclusions were drawn from the conflicting reports, students learned to sharpen their critical skills by accessing and evaluating media content, grammar, and form.[2]

Although this topic is no longer current, almost any major issue conveyed in the news can be applied to this lesson. During the U.S. invasion of the Balkan Islands, there were many differing points of view, updates, and accounts of the bombings, casualties, refugee camps, and the like on the Internet. The political uprisings against the World Trade Organization, International Monetary Fund, and biotechnology industry both within and outside the United States present additional educational lessons, as the establishment of the IMC's Web site has offered a different version of "reality" through independent streamed videos. During Campaign 2000, I encouraged my students to embark upon a month-long project whereby they were responsible for acquiring information about the major presidential candidates as well as third-party candidates, such as Ralph Nader, who received short shrift in the mainstream media. Unlike the mainstream media's "image-based" coverage between Al Gore and George W. Bush, the Internet allowed students to dig deeper into the relevant policies, issues, and visions of competing candidates, allowing them to then create their own "media event" through a collegewide forum based on the new facts and insight they had received online. Students sent out press releases for the event and were pleased to receive media coverage from the local cable access channel as well as from the leading local newspaper. This enabled them to put into practice their media production skills so that they could use their insight to inform others about the issues important to them. Moreover, the activity provided students with a final evaluation of the event as they experienced it, which contrasted sharply with the packaged soundbites and photographs of the mainstream newspaper owned by the *New York Times*.

The problematic news coverage of the ballot-counting in Florida and the protests during the George W. Bush inauguration are also ripe for this kind of critical analysis and evaluation of mainstream and non-mainstream media sources. Naturally, teachers will need to think about the scope and nature of each lesson according to the subject area taught. In addition to devising and implementing appropriate Internet-based lessons, teachers will need to consider not only what sites and sources interest their constituents, but also what pedagogical strategies complement their learning goals and objectives.

### Cyber-Literacy across Subjects

In light of the growing developments of computer-mediated communications in the classroom, the technological and social changes that have taken place in the United States in the last fifty years are beginning to noticeably impact educational reform across the country and beyond. The Massachusetts Board of Education (1994) states that educational reform is needed in schools so that new technological tools can become standard within every classroom, and so that students can "become skilled at organizing, analyzing and making sense of the vast information they receive in the media."

In order to argue for the integration of "cyber-literacy" into the curriculum, it is important to clearly conceptualize the multidimensional functions of, and possibilities for, media literacy in cyberspace in all subject areas. Across the disciplines, the learning possibilities are endless and can achieve several curriculum objectives. In English/language arts, literary works can be researched and presented in more contemporary form through streamed video as a means of expression. Students can access divergent viewpoints and multiple interpretations of key works online in order to challenge values, ideology, and point of view across lines of race, nationality, ethnicity, gender, class, sexuality, and the like. They can also use the Internet as a means to go beyond pre-determined "classics" to discover new forms of literature. Whereas published texts are exclusive to a privileged few and must go through rigorous reviewers and gatekeepers in the print publishing industry, students can easily publish their own narratives, essays, and poetry online through age- and/or level-appropriate Internet sites. Students interested in publishing online can compare and contrast the economic and political imperatives of the mainstream publishing industry with the online community. This will enable them to better understand how the Internet as a medium allows for literary creativity and merit to emerge outside of the narrowly defined marketing- and profit-driven motives of commercialized mass media. Naturally, students will be able to explore how the global distribution of ideas and literary works is also unique to the Internet as a media form.

In math, concepts including measurement, estimation, quantity, probability, and statistics can all explore the relationship between mathematics and the Internet. This includes a critical analysis of both the (mis)representations of figures in online advertising, for instance, and the social manipulation of statistics within cyberspace, particularly as they apply to child or adolescent Web sites. In order to note the differences between online and traditional mediated technologies, teachers can encourage students to quantify their time spent online. A developed lesson would encourage students to quantify the average amount of time they spend searching for the information they need, the amount of advertising they encounter, the time devoted to both educational and entertainment uses of the Internet, and the like. In terms of a broader medium analysis, students can chart the growth of Internet technologies in order to make inferences about its use based on age, socioeconomic status, gender, race, and the like. With the investments and media mergers of multi–billion dollar corporate giants such as Time Warner and AOL, students can itemize and track the growth of interlocking media enterprises (e.g., Disney's acquisition of search engines like Go.com and the marketing of Disney-related products), the increase of marketing initiatives, and the availability of nondominant information.

In science, knowledge about the fundamental principles of the life, physical, earth/space, and technology sciences can lead to many critical lessons. For example, students can access a myriad of health and environmental Web sites, listserves, and chat rooms detailing various issues that have been ignored or misrepresented in the mainstream media. Accordingly, students can access and evaluate the political and economic factors that determine which scientific endeavors are worth studying, whom are they financed by, and how local and global communities are mobilizing to support or oppose such initiatives. Furthermore, students can study how the medium itself radically alters "who knows what about whom" in terms of displacing traditional power structures. For instance, the relationship between doctors and their patients has been altered with the Internet, as doctors no longer have a monopoly on health-related information. Scientists in all areas can engage in collaborative online research across geographic barriers. In terms of their own abilities to "distribute" the fruitions of their own scientific explorations, students can easily share the results of their research online with their peers across temporal and spatial barriers.

In history, important connections between historical events, themes, and issues can be accessed, compared, and contested between various forms of media, allowing for the discovery of multiple and conflicting perspectives. Learning about the history of the Internet can help students explain and formulate questions about its present-day use, and can serve as an example of how the past both shapes and differs from the present. Learning history through the Internet, as well as learning the history of and about the Internet, can help students understand the process by which individuals and groups develop and work within political, social, economic, cultural, and geographic contexts. Similarly, an understanding of the representation of the importance of events and fundamental concepts in community, regional, national, and world history can be explored online. Among the related questions students can ask are: Whose narratives and perspectives are dominant? Whose are missing and why? and How does the Internet broaden the scope and accounts of history? Such work allows students to examine what forms of history are valued, by whom, and with what exceptions. As with video production, students can produce their own his/herstories online through creative uses of multimedia.

In social studies, the principles outlined in historical documents such as the Declaration of Independence, the Constitution, the Bill of Rights, and so forth can be questioned and challenged through the availability and accessability of the Internet and computer education. Students can assess the ability of the Internet to both empower and inhibit democratic initiatives. On the one hand, the Internet provides a more level playing field whereby large amounts of capital are not needed to produce and disseminate messages to a global mass audience. On the other hand, access to online technology and sufficient educational training is unevenly distributed across socioeconomic and generational lines. Discussions can help students determine whether or not access to equal mediated (re)presentations constitutes a basic human right and problematize the possibility for such policy in privately owned media. Additionally, students can explore the controversies that emerge when balancing First Amendment rights with regulation of the Internet by varied parties. With increased monopolistic control of the Internet by large corporations, students can weigh the public's right to know and ability to provide information freely against issues of corporate control of information.

In geography, learning the importance of location and place, demographic trends and patterns, and the relationship between people and the environment can all be achieved online. For instance, unlike the carefully selected locations, scenes, or settings used by the mainstream media to alter perceptions of a people, culture, or country, students can expand their understanding of various cultures and areas by perusing Web sites from around the world. Students can discover demographic trends and patterns, as well as political and economic issues affecting various cultures/regions through personalized electronic correspondence with other students.

Perhaps one of the best ways to learn and understand the nature of the creative process, the characteristics of visual art, music, dance, and theater, and their importance in shaping and reflecting historical and cultural heritage, is through contemporary multimedia. Students can start by analyzing the aesthetic and physiological distinctions between traditional media and online technology. Subsequently, they can examine how cyber-museums, cyber-theater, cyber-concerts, and online local exhibits expand access to the arts. Basic visual and graphic arts components can be used to design Web pages. What's more, students can examine how emerging multimedia are used for personal growth and enjoyment, and with what effects.

In health, the mass media are undoubtedly the primary definers of our basic concepts of human development, mental health, sexuality, parenting, physical education and fitness, nutrition and disease prevention, and understanding the implications of health habits for self and society. Accordingly, the Internet presents many useful lessons whereby students can examine (1) how online advertisements, Web sites, and listserves affect our understanding of these concepts; (2) how certain forms of sexuality are easily exploitable online; (3) how online research can expose the manipulative ways in which sexual pleasure, disease, nutrition, and exercise are balanced through contradictions in commercial media (e.g., eat Stuffed Crust pizza at Pizza Hut, lose weight through Dexatrim, and drink Ensure to maintain the right vitamins and minerals). Likewise, issues regarding (re)presentations in the media of violence, tobacco, alcohol, drugs, teen pregnancy, and sexually transmitted disease can be challenged by juxtaposing corporate Web sites aimed at youth with countercultural educational Web sites. Students can produce their own messages through e-zines and other multimedia technology.

Lastly, in sports and recreation, it is important for students to recognize how growing trends in Internet use lead to physical passivity rather than interactivity. By researching various types of sports and recreation online, students can problematize which "mainstream" sports get aired or covered in great detail, why, and with what exclusions. Students can also use the Internet as a means to find up-to-date information about sporting and recreational events typically ignored by the commercial media and can share their own specific recreational endeavors with other enthusiasts.

In determining how to best integrate online technology across subject areas, teachers will undoubtedly be the best determiners of how to successfully incorporate critical cyber-learning ventures into the curriculum. To use the Internet simply for the sake of laying claims to using technology is not enough if we are to adequately prepare students to become critically autonomous within cyberspace and society at large. Hence more detailed curricular units will need to be developed so that students receive the best "driver education" for their excursions onto the information superhighway.

## FROM CLASSROOMS TO VIRTUAL CYBER-ROOMS: THINKING ABOUT PEDAGOGY AND INTERNET TECHNOLOGY

One of the challenges facing a triangulated curriculum of media literacy, critical pedagogy, and cultural studies is coming to terms with the outcome of education. Ira Shor (1992) espouses a student-centered learning that does not mistake empowerment for students (or teachers) doing whatever they want in life or in the cultural realm. He explains, "the learning process is negotiated, requiring leadership by the teacher and mutual teacher-student authority" (p. 15). Shor doesn't believe in an individualistic empowerment, but uses John Dewey's (1985) notion of civic welfare, or democracy, as the end-all mode of empowerment. For me, the direction of the learning process is less clear. As "civic life" and "democracy" become more individualistic, consumer-oriented interpellations, it is becoming more and more difficult to conceptualize and advance meaningful connections to student needs, interests, and community cultures in a societal climate that cultivates the status quo, consumption, and resistance to participation in any public or philanthropic form. With emerging technologies reflecting the motivations of the corporate business sector through blatant and discrete advertising and marketing ploys, the creative possibilities for interactive participation envisioned by Dewey and Shor seem easily thwarted. This makes the need for student-centered pedagogies more urgent.

Furthermore, Shor's notion of "empowerment" is predicated on the assumption that students are—or can be—motivated through the learning process, thereby leading students to become invested in their own self-transformation, as well as in broad social action and change. Yet the process of "empowering" students can be debilitating for a variety of reasons. First, regardless of teacher intentions and student energies, critical thinking and social activism remain confined by the regimented institution of schooling, where power, authority, tracking, and standardized testing reward individualism, competition, and upward mobility to those who acquiesce to academic rituals. Relatedly, the confines of the school make it difficult for teachers and students to practice and apply learning outside the classroom walls. Regimented time slots for assigned subjects or courses compartmentalize knowledge and application rather than providing learning initiatives with adequate time, careful planning, development, and synthesis. Even the shortness of the academic term or semester, as well as the move toward high-stakes testing, reduce the potential for "empowerment" by stifling deep critical analysis *and* application.

When introducing students to nondominant ideologies and historical analyses charting the interconnections between the media, big business, and the U.S. government, I see my students become angry, uncomfortable, and energized. While I cannot lay claims to the "empowerment" of *all* students, nor do I aspire to, the shortness of the semester and structure of academe create an anticlimactic denouement at the end of the semester for those students who do wish to apply their learning outside the classroom. It does not take long for "empowered" students to become *dis*empowered when they begin their quest for employment in a world where "marketable skills" are both preferred and financially rewarded over "critical skills." This is not to say that learning does not lead students to build coalitions with other students and groups, but that the overall level of "empowerment" is daunting for those who understand the insurmountable odds and structures present within and outside the institution of schooling.[3]

Beyond the structural limitations obscuring the facility of student "empowerment" are philosophical concerns regarding the conceptualizations of critical pedagogy—from which a host of underlying presumptions emerge about the possibilities for change through student voice, dialogue, democracy, and power. Elizabeth Ellsworth (1989) takes on the limits of critical pedagogy by denouncing the level of abstraction that emerges from concepts of freedom, justice, democracy, and "universal" values. As she explains, the theoretical constructs within critical pedagogy must be clearly articulated by thinking through and planning classroom practices to support the political agenda of any course:

> When educational researchers advocating critical pedagogy fail to provide a clear statement of their political agendas, the effect is to hide the fact that as critical pedagogues, they are in fact seeking to appropriate public resources (classrooms, school supplies, teacher/professor salaries, academic requirements and degrees) to further various "progressive" political agendas that they believe to be for the public good—and therefore deserving of public resources. (p. 93)

Accordingly, the goals, priorities, risks, and potentials developing from critical pedagogy need to be clearly articulated. In my own teaching, the goal is to win semiotic space for marginalized discourses surrounding the use, structure, and commercial implications of Internet technology. Rather than assume that rational deliberation through teacher/student dialogue and expression will lead toward truth through equally valid competing claims, Ellsworth reminds us that, as critical pedagogues, we should recognize that the voices of students *and* teachers are partial narratives:

> partial in the sense that they are unfinished, imperfect, limited; and partial in the sense that they project the interests of "one side" over others. Because those voices are partial and partisan, they must be made problematic, but not because they have broken the rules of thought of the ideal rational person by grounding their knowledge in immediate emotional, social, and psychic experiences of oppression, or are somehow lacking or too narrowly circumscribed. Rather, they must be critiqued because they hold implications for other social movements and their struggles for self-definition. This assertion carries important implications for the "goal" of classroom practices against oppressive formations. (p. 97)

As previously mentioned, the pedagogical goal of student empowerment tends to be defined in the broadest possible humanistic terms without addressing any identifiable social or political position, institution, or group. Moreover, "emancipatory authority" implies the presence of, or potential for, an emancipated teacher who "can link knowledge to power by bringing to light and teaching the subjugated histories, experiences, stories, and accounts of those who suffer and struggle" (p. 99). Ellsworth points out that no teacher is free from learned and internalized oppressions. Thus, although literature recognizes that teachers have much to learn from their students' experiences, it does not address the ways in which professors/teachers can

> *never know* about the experiences, oppressions, and understandings of other participants in the class. This situation makes it impossible for any single voice in the classroom—including that of the professor—to assume the position of center or origin of knowledge or authority, of having privileged access to authentic experience or appropriate language. A recognition, contrary to all Western ways of knowing and speaking, that all knowings are partial, that there are fundamental things each of us cannot know—a situation alleviated only in part by the pooling of partial, socially constructed knowledges in classrooms—demands a fundamental retheorizing of "education" and "pedagogy." (pp. 101–102)

This level of retheorizing is not meant to stifle the teacher's role as scholar and educator, but to make explicit the partiality of any teleological assumption about knowledge, even within critical pedagogy.

In addition to the problem of assuming an authentic "voice," from which students and teachers can freely and equally speak, Ellsworth takes apart conventional notions of dialogue and democracy that assume that rationalized, individualized subjects can agree on universalizable "fundamental moral principles" and "quality of human life" (p. 108). First, social agents cannot assume to be fully rational and disinterested, as varied social positionings divide people into complex subjects. Second, fundamental moral and political principles are established intersubjectively by subjects capable of interpretations and reflection (p. 108). Accordingly, "educational researchers attempting to construct meaningful discourses about the politics of classroom practices must begin to theorize the consequences for education of the ways knowledge, power and desire are mutually implicated in each other's formations and deployments" (p. 108).

Given these limits of critical pedagogy, it is necessary to examine its terms and philosophy when working to address media literacy and cyberspace. As Ellsworth reminds us, power and subjectivity influence all classroom dynamics. At the heart of cyberspace exploration in schools is the need to go beyond traditional democratic ideals of equal access to information and technology. Teachers and students need to become "problem-posers" by interrogating how new technologies create inequuities according to socioeconomic status, education, gender, age, and the like. Using Dewey's notion of "democracy" as a broad experiential condition where the needs of individuals *and* society are cultivated, schools need to devise pedagogical strategies to address those complicated structures of power that set people up as unequal members of society through new technologies (Itzkoff, 1969).

Although such strategies should not assume consensus or immediate transformative possibilities, teachers and administrators should expose the politics involved in this kind of power struggle. This requires asking difficult questions that address the computer-information divide (who has the skills and access to use the Internet), how the "civic arena" is redefined through decentralized technology, and whether silences and resistance to, or a conscious disengagement from, the "civic arena" constitute a different kind of participation through new communication technologies.

The lessons provided here are a starting point, a beginning from which multiple learning opportunities can be developed, adapted, reconfigured, and altered so that students and teachers tackle the difficulties of addressing the decline of cultural pluralism in all areas of social life, including the realm of new information technologies. An especially important area from which the politics of cultural pluralism can be explored is media production. Not only is critical analysis vital to the study and utilization of new technologies, but media production is vital to all pedagogy. Just as it is necessary for students to learn to write as well as to read, it is invaluable for teachers to allow students to "produce" media texts as well as deconstruct them through their own voice, ideas, and perspective (realizing of course the partial subjectivity from which these voices emanate). As Gayatri Spivak (1989) explains, deconstruction is not about an exposure of error, but is "a way of thinking . . . about the danger of what is powerful and useful" (cited in Lather, 1991, p. 13). Citing John Caputo (1987), Patti Lather (1991) explains that the goal of deconstructive critique is "to keep things in process, to disrupt, to keep the system in play, to set up procedures to continuously demystify the realities we create, to fight the tendency for our categories to congeal" (p. 13). Lather elaborates:

> Deconstruction foregrounds the lack of innocence in any discourse by looking at the textual staging of knowledge, the constitutive efforts of our uses of language. As the postmodern equivalent of the dialectic, deconstruction provides a corrective moment, a safeguard against dogmatism, a continual displacement. (p. 13)

Although I would agree with David Sholle and Stan Denski (1994) that many liberal arts programs tend to reproduce the market logic of capitalism in their media/video production courses, as well as in computer software applications and Web-page design, I believe that as teachers, we need to accept student locations both within and outside the dominant culture, allowing students to determine what a "new" vision or new (re)presentation should or could look like—not only as individuals, but also as individuals occupying multiple subject positions from which they can locate themselves in relation to others. In other words, to simply show students how to deconstruct ideology or showing them examples of "alternative" productions or sources of information is not enough to transform those structures of knowledge and power that consume us (although the positions of the left are less predominant within the media than mainstream or conservative positions, they are nevertheless part of the ideological).[4] While not all students may be in a position to determine "new" visions, teachers will need to work with students in developing a pedagogy that goes beyond reproducing or maintaining the status quo, thereby leading to social change and cultural actions.

Since we are never outside power, it would make more sense to let students develop their critical visions and understandings of power structures within the media through their experimentations with media production. I like to think of this process as one in which students learn to take apart ideology, just as one would take apart the pieces of a puzzle, with the freedom and ability to re-create a new picture or puzzle through their own (re)assembling of the parts. This (re)assembling process is further aided by new technologies allowing students to easily-cut and paste, digitally edit, and manipulate media forms. As Kathleen Tyner (1998) suggests, the key is to stress the manipulation of technology tools by students, so that they become information providers as well as receivers.

Accordingly, there is something uniquely powerful about combining both analysis and production, as it allows us to explore pedagogical possibilities through alternative media. Video production is only one of several means through which students can learn to "talk back" or respond to/through the media. Role play, collage, journals, and computer applications present other possibilities. In terms of the Internet, a production component to cyber-education provides students with the right skills necessary to explore, interrogate, and/or analyze how the media define our world, shape our culture, are politically and economically organized, and can be reorganized and rearranged in new ways. Since the only way to transform or intervene in power networks of communication is to reciprocate through other communication networks, students will need to learn how to design Web pages, correspond through e-mail, and use multimedia to develop and present their critical cultural capacities.

Through a pedagogy of risk and articulation, Ira Shor (1992) and Lawrence Grossberg (1994) both maintain that, although teachers must go beyond traditional notions of intellectual authority, they do not have to dismiss claims to authority. Naturally, the teacher plays a critical role in the classroom due to her/his experience and proficiencies in the subject area(s) taught. But if the main pedagogy motivating the educational process is a discursive flow of interactions between students and teachers, students and students, and students and society, knowledge and the learning process are "multiply created." Accordingly, more Web-based lessons like those designed in this chapter need to be created so that teachers work to amalgamate potentially transformative possibilities instead of dispensing all knowledge.

I will conclude by noting that a media literacy pedagogy of risk and articulation is even more vital to secondary school programs if we assume that those who go on to college have learned to "master" those ideological knowledge forms structuring education and are most likely attending school voluntarily. For "at-risk" youth dismayed by traditional approaches to learning at the secondary level, media production allows them to use their creativity, experience, and vision to create rather than regurgitate knowledge forms already determined valuable by the teacher/culture. To go beyond a "vocational approach" (whereby students simply learn to mimic production values and aesthetics determined by the market) would allow students to produce video pieces and Web pages that affect them and in which they are invested.[5]

In the end, media literacy curriculum materials and pedagogical designs will need to include the use of new information technologies so that teachers are provided with innovative and high-quality education programs that enable them and their students to expand their conceptualization and application of critical literacy skills as both autonomous individuals and social beings. The following conclusion will address the limits and contributions, as well as the future direction, of media education initiatives in cyberspace.

## NOTES

1. America Online has already been charged with using filters to block out several Web sites associated with liberal political organizations. One of the top stories featured in Censored 2001 was AOL's liberal blacklist, whereby sites for the Democratic National Committee, Ralph Nader's Green Party, Ross Perot's Reform Party, the Coalition to Stop Gun Violence, and Safer Guns Now were labeled as "not appropriate for children" (Phillips, 2001, p. 111). Ironically, the youth filters did not prevent access to nudity or to conservative groups including the National Rifle Association. Designed for America Online by The Learning Company, an educational software company owned by Mattel, such filtering programs confirm suspicions about the process of labeling Web sites according to political and economic interests.

2. Dr. Renee Hobbs uses a similar activity by inviting secondary school teachers participating in the Re-Visioning Project (1998) to look at several different Web sites about the assassination of John F. Kennedy in order to devise and utilize analytical Internet skills.

3. Without a doubt, a renewed level of student mobilization and coalition building was witnessed in the Seattle, Washington, protests of December 1999, where students coordinated their demonstrative efforts against the World Trade Organization and successfully stymied talks by international board members. Nonetheless, many students are easily frustrated by their inability to partake in such events due to their work and parental responsibilities, as well as concerns about travel, physical harm, and police arrests.

4. Showing alternatives to slick, commercially produced media forms is nonetheless essential to teaching students the implications and wide-ranging potential of media production, so long as the politics of this pedagogical initiative are disclosed.

5. This notion of learning comes from an article on the Educational Video Center (EVC) in New York, which offers high school credit to students who do not "succeed" in traditional educational settings (EVC, 120W 30th Street, New York, NY 10001; e-mail: www.evc.org).

# Conclusion

In the initial chapters, we began by posing questions aimed at investigating what administrative, educational, and parental concerns affect the implementation of online technology in the classroom. Through a search of mainstream print and online media sources, we began to summarize and draw from the polemic surrounding Internet technology in the classroom. Accordingly, our findings suggest that "inappropriate content" constitutes a cultural currency through which concerns and responses to the Internet have been articulated within the mainstream. As such, the cultural response to such narratives has proffered inoculation or regulation through forces of government or market control. By focusing on objections to market control of the Internet, the political countercharge to these measures has ensued in an individualized, rather than organizational or systemic, mobilization of citizens, so that the "safeguarding" of minors from "objectionable" Internet material has fallen onto the shoulders of concerned parents.

Not surprisingly, third-party shielding systems designed to prevent children or youth from selecting and responding to "offensive" content have proliferated. Rooted in inoculative tactics, software companies have designed "customer-driven" parental blocking devices to prefilter Internet content through designated trigger words, third-party rating systems, and warning labels. Left aside from these propositions are the problematic consequences of these regulatory measures. Although government regulation has been decried as undercutting free speech, the control of Internet content through capitalist gateways—namely profit-driven software companies—has gone largely uncriticized. Such a discursive trend manufactures consent through a hegemonic force neglecting to confront the invasion of online advertising or marketing strategies directed at children. In addition to evaluating three Web sites (SafeSurf, Net Nanny, and CyberPatrol) and several related links recommended or selected by third-party rating systems as well as software filtering products, we need to examine the rhetorical and financial investments of the telecommunications business sector that emanate from endorsements of, and partnerships with, the Recreational Software Advisory Council on the Internet (RSACi). Moreover, we need to be critical of the rhetorical elements that create cyber-paranoia within the mainstream in an attempt to reach the consent of parents and educators by asking them to see some Internet content as value-laden (nudity, sexuality, trigger words, or adult content), while disguising the interests and authority of profitable computer software and hardware industries (advertising and marketing). As this study indicates, we need to expound and inspire a vision for concrete curricular proposals leading to critical inquiry-based learning in cyberspace.

In order to strengthen such a vision, we assessed the technology initiatives in Massachusetts schools sponsored through the Lighthouse Technology Grants. Although the hope was to discover curricular projects employing some aspects of media literacy, the results indicate that no such approaches (in)formed the educational thrust of the funded programs. Using the major categories of Bloom's cognitive domain of the taxonomy of educational objectives (1956), we discovered that the Lighthouse Grants focused primarily on knowledge, comprehension, and application. Technology-based activities (software programs, computer games, CD-ROMs, or Internet data) were mainly used to reinforce previously learned skills or material. Subsequently, the higher levels of learning essential for critical media literacy (analysis, synthesis, and evaluation) went largely undeveloped.

Drawing from Osborne and Freyberg (1985) and Bransford and Vye (1989), it became evident that the types of projects funded through the technology grants did not radically deviate from a non-technology-based curriculum. Moreover, our findings indicate that the Lighthouse Grants did not encourage students to reflect upon and judge (analyze and evaluate) the veracity and sociopolitical implications of the materials acquired through telecommunications technology, CD-ROMs, software programs, or computer games. Since the production elements associated with the use of video and multimedia did not significantly alter (or synthesize) the content of the materials being presented, the conclusions suggest that the curricular drive of effective classroom learning can be better conceptualized and adapted through communications technology if a media literacy component is added.

In addition to the Lighthouse Grants, this study indicates that two additional "EdTech" programs supported by the Massachusetts Department of Education need examination. The first, the Virtual High School (VHS) project, is designed to create and convey academic content through the Internet. Although some of the VHS programs offer pedagogically rich capacities by taking learning outside classroom walls, this program extends or alters the *means* of education without impacting the *content*. Likewise, the second study examined, the Youth Tech Entrepreneurs (YTE), emphasizes the lower tiers of Bloom's taxonomy by containing application through interdistrict and community business technology support services. Although the Massachusetts Department of Education extols the benefits of such programs as curricular reform, the promotion of practical rather than cognitive computer skills privileges a market-driven education system. Hence, the integration of technology and learning must go beyond a mastery of computer skills or proficiencies so that students can better acquire the competence needed to become lifelong learners.

With few models offering higher levels of critical learning *with* and *about* technology, we explored the need for a model of educational empowerment over censorship through the theoretical and practical considerations of media literacy in cyberspace. Using Joshua Meyrowitz's explanation of multiple media literacies (1998), the undergirding of an online information literacy design can be articulated through four phases or types of media literacy: media content literacy, media grammar literacy, medium literacy, and institutional analysis. By offering these multiple literacies as a means through which to conceive of curricular lessons and projects, we can design and construct a vision for the development of critical literacy skills in cyberspace. Not only is this design theoretically grounded, but it also develops and outlines four hands-on experiential examples of cyber-literacy lessons applicable to educational environments.

## FITTING CYBER-LITERACY INTO THE CURRICULUM

Although the literature has been sparse and has proposed models insufficient to address the challenges presented by the emergence of new information technologies in schools and other learning environments, serious thought needs to be devoted to the multidimensional opportunities and problems presented by digital technology. Through the conglomeration of media literacy, classroom pedagogy, and curricular issues centered around technological access *and* critical evaluation, we've been able to provide evidence for, and strategies designed to deal with, educational technology.

Many teachers and critical pedagogues have criticized the field of communications study for its inability to inform contemporary education practices within elementary and secondary curricular programs. In response to this deficiency, we've demonstrated the need for both a theoretical and a pragmatic foundation that provide hands-on learning lessons encouraging knowledge "about" and "through" new information technologies. Moreover, while much communication and educational research focuses on the effective (or ineffective) application of new information technologies to the improvement of reading or writing comprehension, as well as other standard competencies, we need to continue to challenge the very essence of the learning process by critiquing those institutional forces aiming to offer a packaged curriculum through marketable skills rather than creative curricular applications.

In the 1998 special media literacy issue of the *Journal of Communication*, Christ and Potter highlighted the importance of posing three main questions associated with curriculum, all of which apply to both K–12 and higher education (p. 8). They are: (1) What is the purpose of the curriculum? (2) How should media literacy fit into the curriculum? and (3) What are the key elements or principles of media literacy that should be taught? It is through the questioning of school culture that pedagogical models will be designed to restructure the learning process as well as the curricular content. By encouraging teachers to be more flexible in determining the process and outcome of the learning experience, the methods herein allow teachers to guide students through the effective use of group dialogue and questioning strategies, thereby encouraging students to (a) be pensively deliberative, (b) synthesize concepts and ideas, and (c) critically interrogate the political, economic, and symbiotic factors impacting media and society.

Relatedly, while the field of educational technology has emerged in response to the growing realization that teachers are using more audiovisual and information technology, this research delineates a hybrid area of study through its focus on the critical uses of electronic forms of literacy, not for the sake of technology alone, but for the purposes of providing students with lifelong literacy skills (Tyner, 1998, p. 58). Even among the limited resources delineating a Web-based curriculum, few consider the curricular ideas and strategies espoused in this study, nor do they address the higher levels of cognitive development that lead to an understanding of the signification of meaning.

## CYBER-VENTURES INTO THE FUTURE

Despite the findings and gains procured by the present research, further excursions are necessary to continue to address the importance of developing media literacy in cyberspace. First, a comprehensive account of the current uses of educational technology is necessary in order to discover additional local, national, and global media literacy approaches and practices. Although the Lighthouse Technology Grants and EdTech projects provide some understanding of the multicurricular projects employed throughout schools in Massachusetts, other programs in the United States and abroad would need to be appraised in order to effectively determine and draw from the array of critically based technology lessons. Upon the location of such programs, future research should include direct classroom observations as well as case studies pertaining to the application and evaluation of computer technologies. Furthermore, the assessment of learning gains, as well as of student resistance, is also necessary in continuing research in this area.

As Kathleen Tyner (1998) explains, "many more perspectives are needed to shape the debate about the specific uses of new and emerging communications technologies if teaching and learning are to be responsive to students who live in a world awash with information" (p. 71). Accordingly, coalitions and alliances between educators, public leaders, and citizens are needed in order for some consensus to evolve about the role of technology within and outside education.

Like Tyner, Howard Rheingold (1994) resolves that the political significance of computer-managed communications "lies in its capacity to challenge the existing political hierarchy's monopoly on powerful communications media, and perhaps thus revitalize citizen-based democracy" (p. 14). With large, multinational corporations swallowing up small, independent media firms and communications technologies, new ways must be devised to take control over those privately owned cultural arenas that threaten our ability to access information freely and become independent cultural producers. Otherwise, just as big power and big money always found ways to control new communications media when they emerged in the past, the odds are always good that they will find a way to control access to virtual communities (p. 4–5). As we've demonstrated, this has already taken place, making calls for action indispensable.

Consequently, if computer technologies are to live up to their potential, more people must learn about and learn how to effectively use the Internet while there is still limited freedom to do so. If teachers, administrators, parents, and citizens care deeply about the future of the medium that enables us to assemble worldwide through computer conferencing and home pages, we will need to reconsider educational theories and practices designed to include new technologies in schools.

Rather than letting the ruling ideological "concerns" over censorship and inappropriate content on the Internet overtake the very means enabling us to take part in culture and society, we need to sharpen and employ the critical competencies we need to resist, take pleasure from, and create values and meanings from emerging information technologies. As suggested in this study, this means going beyond the acceptance of prefiltered computer software and hardware products devised by financially motivated computer industries. Since today's students will only become more deeply entangled within a "Web" of information with the continual proliferation of new technologies, further research is needed in media literacy, critical pedagogy, and cultural studies to ensure that students are taught to intelligently assess, survey, and wield communications technology as they prepare to become society's future citizenry.

# 1998–1999 Massachusetts Lighthouse Technology Grants: Project Summaries

### Language Arts: Fourteen projects

1. Students enhance writing abilities through portfolios.

2. Enhanced reading/writing—connecting to subject matter, authors, and events through Internet use, creating stories through various software (evaluating and making choices about the various types of media available to them).

3. Program "Wiggle Works" used to promote early literacy—students produce their own books using technology.

4. Middle school students create Hyperstudio presentations relating to topics from the eighth-grade language arts curriculum designed to integrate with technology (cross-listed under Technology).

5. Technology used to address verbal literacy through alternative methods for high school students with special needs (cross-listed under Technology).

6. Online student magazines created at high school level to integrate both telecommunications and language arts curriculum (cross-listed under Technology).

7. Sixth-grade social studies and language arts students use computer software, CD-ROMs, and the Internet to make connections between their ancestors and U.S. and world histories (cross-listed under Social Studies).

8. Technology incorporated into the writing process for elementary school writers to improve organization, sequence, research, and language mechanics and develop finished stories and reports.

9. Sixth-grade students engage in learning grammar through a teacher-designed computer-based program that color-codes sentence parts.

10. Kindergarten through twelfth-grade students use AVID cinema desktop video technology to create original work and learn to speak and write clearly for a specific audience (cross-listed under Technology).

11. Sixth-grade students serve as "literacy buddies" for first-graders, helping them publish their books and drawings with computers and scanners.

12. First- and fourth-graders work together as "study buddies" or student mentors using technology to help students become better writers.

13. Technology is used as a vehicle for research to encourage elementary school teachers to develop lessons for collecting information and ideas on a Web site dealing with the three ways children's literature can be utilized to stimulate multicultural discussions in the elementary school classroom.

14. Students in multi-age first- and second-grade use software program Kid Pix to create individual slides based on research projects in language arts.

## Technology: Nine projects

1. Middle school students use Sim City 2000 simulation software to meet state curriculum standards on cities.

2. Middle school students create Hyperstudio presentations relating to topics from the eighth-grade language arts curriculum designed to integrate with technology (cross-listed under Language Arts).

3. Technology used to address verbal literacy through alternative methods for high school students with special needs (cross-listed under Language Arts).

4. Maintenance of school district Web site and training offered to teachers and students to use the Internet as a publishing tool (internship).

5. Online student magazines created at high school level to integrate both telecommunications and language arts curriculum (cross-listed under Language Arts).

6. Seventh through twelfth-grade science and technology students study biotechnology, lasers, telecommunications, environmental technology, and robotics (cross-listed under Science).

7. Kindergarten through twelfth-grade students use AVID cinema desktop video technology to create original work and learn to speak and write clearly for a specific audience (cross-listed under Language Arts).

8. Kindergarten through eighth-grade students at the Science and Technology Magnet School use computers and labs for projects using technology for research, data collection, problem solving, communicating ideas, and discourse with other students and professionals (cross-listed under Science).

9. High school students use industry standard drafting software to better understand architectural styles, structure, and neighborhood development.

## Science: Twelve projects

1. Students use program LEGO/DACTA to build and program their own machines.

2. Technology integrated into the teaching of physics in ninth grade to learn the state standards on force, motion, energy, light, and sound.

3. Students collect and share data on species and habitats through online data collection at the Concord Consortium, graphing calculators, e-mail, bulletin boards, and other applications.

4. Middle school students study the physics of sailing, hydro- and aerodynamics, ocean ecology, and world cultures through a ten-month program; data is collected and shared through a biweekly newspaper, video portfolio, and Web pages (cross-listed under Social Studies).

5. Seventh-graders work in teams and in canoes on a three-day trip that studies the Ipswich River and its ecosystems; eighth-grade students take a multimedia approach to studying the history of Ipswich and prepare presentations for the Ipswich Historical Society (cross-listed under Social Studies).

6. Technology incorporated into the teaching of math where it is needed in physics (cross-listed under Math).

7. Sixth- and seventh-graders use technology to work collaboratively to solve a design challenge requiring math and physical science concepts (cross-listed under Math).

8. Seventh through twelfth-grade science and technology students study biotechnology, lasers, telecommunications, environmental technology, and robotics (cross-listed under Technology).

9. At-risk and advanced fourth-grade students use the latest technology to research black inventors (cross-listed under Social Studies).

10. Third- and fourth-graders use technology to conduct scientific investigations of local water samples; they analyze the data, write reports, summarize their findings, deliver electronic presentations of their work, and exchange e-mail with students in Shutesbury engaged in a parallel investigation.

11. Kindergarten through eighth-grade students at the Science and Technology Magnet School use computers and labs for projects using technology for research, data collection, problem solving, communicating ideas, and discourse with other students and professionals (cross-listed under Technology).

12. Elementary school students use technology to study the school's outdoor environment by creating maps, field guides, and databases of plant and animal species, which they publish on the Web.

## Social Studies: Eight projects

1. Government and historical materials available over the Internet used to enhance engaging the social studies curriculum in "real" tasks and "real" issues connecting to classroom topics.

2. Web-based curriculum materials designed by teachers and museum professionals brought into the classroom through a "history museum."

3. Sixth-grade social studies and language arts students use computer software, CD-ROMs, and the Internet to make connections between their ancestors and U.S. and world histories (cross-listed under Language Arts).

4. Students come up with questions at the beginning of each new historical or literary unit and then use the Internet to hunt for information, evaluate and compare answers, and report findings.

5. Middle school students study the physics of sailing, hydro- and aerodynamics, ocean ecology, and world cultures through a ten-month program; data is collected and shared through a biweekly newspaper, video portfolio, and Web pages (cross-listed under Science).

6. Seventh-graders work in teams and in canoes on a three-day trip that studies the Ipswich River and its ecosystems; eighth-grade stu-

dents take a multimedia approach to studying the history of Ipswich and prepare presentations for the Ipswich Historical Society (cross-listed under Science).

7. Third- and fourth-graders collect data on Massachusetts geography, government, history, and economy for entry into a database to be shared with other students who have collected similar information on their states.

8. At-risk and advanced fourth-grade students use the latest technology to research black inventors (cross-listed under Science).

## Math: Six projects

1. Biodiversity data collection.

2. Elementary students design and construct interactive math Web sites that other students can access on the Internet.

3. Third- and fourth-grade students use computers to play math games that reinforce math skills (before school begins).

4. Technology incorporated into the teaching of math where it is needed in physics (cross-listed under Science).

5. Sixth- and seventh-graders use technology to work collaboratively to solve a design challenge requiring math and physical science concepts (cross-listed under Science).

6. Third-graders use technology and software programs to learn math skills.

## Business: Four projects

1. Key Pal Community & Business Connections for Middle Grades: students matched with mentors from local businesses and use e-mail communication software to collaborate with mentors on curriculum-based projects aligned with state frameworks.

2. High school seniors use technology to build a portfolio of their work experiences from a five-week School-to-Work internship program; in addition to the use of daily journal entries and electronic time sheets, students prepare electronic slide-show presentations to share with other students.

3. Tenth- through twelfth-grade students complete design projects using state-of-the-art design techniques for clients from the business communities in their school districts.

4. Twelfth-grade students use the latest technology to research investment options, create and maintain portfolios, track the performance of markets and companies, and participate in an online stock market investment game.

## Art/Graphic Design: Four projects

1. Fifth-grade students use technology to research artists whose work is displayed at the Boston Museum of Fine Arts.
2. Ninth-grade students research an art movement using technology and books and write a collaborative paper; upon presentation of the reports, a director oversees the production of a logo/marketing package for an imaginary client using the style of art they researched.
3. Visual arts and music students use technology to digitize known and original works and combine them by responding interpretively to the other discipline's creations (cross-listed under Music).
4. High schools students use computers in an applied arts program to learn about resolution, color separation, file formats, and various media outputs.

## Music: Two projects

1. A Music Technology Lab enables students in grades nine through twelve to learn composition, transcribing, arranging, and transposing in addition to the basics of musical notation, ear training, and rhythm.
2. Music and visual arts students use technology to digitize known and original works and combine them by responding interpretively to the other discipline's creations (cross-listed under Art/Graphic Design).

## Special Education: Two projects

1. Multisensory learning opportunities provided for special-needs and non-special-needs students in prekindergarten, kindergarten, and elementary classrooms.
2. Deaf and hard-of-hearing students work collaboratively with hearing students to produce and direct the filming of videotapes using special software and hardware to edit and create the final captioned videos.

## ESL (English as a second language): One project

1. Sixth- through eighth-grade students develop their English vocabulary using Hyperstudio.

## Foreign Language: Two projects

1. Kindergarten through twelfth-grade students produce videos primarily in a foreign language using research, scripts, storyboards, video cameras, audio mixers, VCRs, and computer editing software.
2. Bilingual students are linked with other schools in the United States and Vietnam for the purpose of developing authentic instructional materials and improving communication and subject area skills.

## Interdisciplinary Programs: Thirteen projects

1. Seventh-graders use technology to capture images and gather data from their backyards to help them identify how their yards are unique, yet part of the global community.
2. Eighth-graders use the latest technology to research multiculturalism, create and prepare cultural dishes from their cultural backgrounds, research and write essays on their cultures using the Internet, and prepare multimedia presentations for the class.
3. Prekindergarten through fifth-grade students publish poetry, stories, science projects, maps, artwork, and more to the school's Web site.
4. Middle school students use computer work stations to study music and its relationship to math and science, use video to link their studies in algebra, geometry, and measurements concepts to theater arts, and use the Internet to study geography and ancient history.
5. Seventh- through twelfth-grade students use a Web site created as a cross-curriculum project that integrates language arts, literature, social studies, mathematics, technology, and the vocational arts.
6. Fifth-grade students work with first-graders to enhance language arts, math, science, social studies, and presentation skills through the use of technology.

7. Sixth-graders prepare research projects, combining note-taking and information literacy skills from language arts with content material from science and social studies to create a Hyperstudio audiovisual presentation for parents and other students.

8. Walpole senior citizens share their personal experiences of history with fourth-grade students through a regular e-mail exchange to enhance students' English/language arts skills; live video conferencing with the senior center allows students to ask prepared questions based on their social studies unit.

9. Students in grades nine through twelve produce infomercials that highlight schoolwide or community projects for Ware's television channel 3 and in-house access channel; students use their skills in English/language arts, visual arts, and computer-assisted design to produce multimedia presentations that combine three-dimensional animated graphics, music, and voice.

10. High school students with special needs, in foster care, or at risk receive assisted or tutored individual lessons in a small-group instructional setting in the Technology and Project Challenge Lab; assessment includes portfolios, process-oriented outcomes, and observable improvement in the areas of math, science, language arts, and fine arts.

11. Integrated curriculum work in grades six through eight enhances the learning of students through improved uses of technology; students use the Internet to study inspirational figures such as Henry David Thoreau, Rachel Carson, and Dr. Martin Luther King Jr., as well as research and design Web pages.

12. Use of the Internet allows for an eight-week multidisciplinary unit based on the Iditarod dogsled race, enabling third-graders to combine learning about Alaska, its land, and its peoples with the challenges of the race; students visit the official Iditarod Web site, conduct research, e-mail questions to mushers, and communicate with keypals on a daily basis.

13. Grant used to participate in Virtual High School (VHS), where students learn in a technology-rich environment while participating in courses offered over the Internet.


**Assessment: Two projects**

1. Technology is used to support and disseminate student assessment practices that enlist second-grade students in reflecting on and directing their own learning and teachers in improving their class-

room instruction in math and reading; students use videotaped presentations and interviews.

2. Technology is used to archive student work and create interactive CD-ROM–based multimedia portfolios as an ongoing assessment and individual curriculum planning tool.

# APPENDIX B

# Bloom's Cognitive Domain of the Taxonomy of Educational Objectives

1. *Knowledge*. The ability to recall previously learned material.
2. *Comprehension*. The ability to grasp the meaning of material; the ability to translate material from one form to another (e.g., words to numbers), explain and summarize material, and predict effects or consequences.
3. *Application*. The ability to use learned material in new situations.
4. *Analysis*. The ability to break down material into its component parts; includes identifying the parts, analyzing the relationship among the parts, and recognizing the organizational principles involved.
5. *Synthesis*. The ability to put parts together to form a new whole (writing a theme, creating a speech, etc.).
6. *Evaluation*. The ability to judge the value of material based on specific criteria.

# References

Adorno, T. W., & Horkheimer, M. (1972). *The dialectic of enlightenment.* (1947). New York: Continuum.

Agger, B. (1992). *Cultural studies as critical theory.* London and Washington, DC: Falmer Press.

Althusser, L. (1971). Ideology and ideological state apparatuses (Notes toward an investigation). In L. Althusser (Ed.), *Lenin and philosophy, and other essays* (pp. 123–173). London: New Left Books.

Alvarado, A., & Boyd-Barrett, O. (Eds.). (1992). *Media education: An introduction.* London: British Film Institute.

Apple, M. (1990). *Ideology and curriculum.* New York: Routledge.

Aronowitz, S. (1992). Looking out: The impact of computers on the lives of professionals. In M. Tuman (Ed.), *Literacy online: The promise (and peril) of reading and writing with computers* (pp. 119–138). Pittsburgh: University of Pittsburgh Press.

Aufderheide, P. (Ed.). (1993). *Media literacy: A report of the national leadership conference on media literacy.* Aspen, CO: Aspen Institute.

Bazalgette, C., Bevort, E., & Savino, J. (Eds.). (1992). *New directions in media education worldwide.* London: British Film Institute.

Becker, H. J. (1995, December). Schools of the National School Network Testbed: Current Internet use. Paper presented at the Fourth International Conference on Telecommunications in Education, Fort Lauderdale, FL.

Birkerts, S. (1994). *The Gutenberg elegies: The fate of reading in an electronic age.* Boston: Faber and Faber.

Bloom, B. S., et al. (1956). *Taxonomy of educational objectives: Cognitive domain.* New York: David McKay.

Bolter, J. D. (1991). *Writing space: The computer, hypertext, and the history of writing.* Hillsdale, NJ: Lawrence Erlbaum.

Bracey, B. (1997). Foreword. In L. Parker Roerden, *Net lessons: Web-based projects for your classroom* (pp. ix–x). Sebastopol, CA: Songline Studios and O'Reilly & Associates.

Bransford, J., & Vye, N. (1989). A perspective on cognitive research and its implications for instruction. In L. Resnick and L. Klopfer (Eds.), *Toward the thinking curriculum: Current cognitive research* (pp. 173–205). Washington, DC: Association for Supervision and Curriculum Development.

Brown, J. A. (1991). *Television "critical viewing skills" education: Major media literacy projects in the United States and selected countries.* Hillsdale, NJ: Lawrence Erlbaum.

———. (1998, Winter). Media literacy perspectives. *Journal of Communication,* 44–57.

Bruce, B. C. (1996). Foreword. In R. Garner & M. G. Gillingham, *Internet communication in six classrooms: conversations across time, space, and culture* (pp. ix–xii). Mahwah, NJ: Lawrence Erlbaum.

Buckingham, D. (1992). Media education: From pedagogy to practice. In M. Alvarado & O. Boyd-Barrett (Eds.), *Media education: An introduction* (pp. 89–91). London: British Film Institute.

———. (1998, Winter). Media education in the UK: Moving beyond protectionism. *Journal of Communication,* 33–43.

——— (Ed.). (1990). *Watching media learning, making sense of media education.* Basingstoke, UK: Falmer Press.

Bundy, A. (1997, 3 August) *Pedagogy, politics, power: Preaching information literacy to the unconverted.* Keynote address on information literacy to the Catholic Teacher Librarians Conference in New South Wales.

Burbules, N. (Forthcoming). Misinformation, malinformation, messed-up information, and mostly useless information: How to avoid getting tangled up in the Net. To appear in Chris Bigum, Colin Lankshear et al. (Eds.), *Digital rhetorics: New technologies, literacy, and learning—Current practices and new directions.* Canberra: Department of Employment, Education, Training, and Youth Affairs, and Brisbane: Queensland University of Technology.

Butterbaugh, S. (1996, June 1). May be unsafe . . . KidsCom service draws data cops' scrutiny. *Cowles Business Media Inc.,* 7(8), 1.

Campbell, J. R., Voelke, K. E., & Donahue, P. L. (1996, November). *Report in brief: NAEP 1994 trends in academic progress.* Princeton: Educational Testing Service, and National Center for Education Statistics.

Campeau, P. L. (1974). Selective review of the results of research on the use of audio-visual media to teach adults. *AV Communication Review,* 22(1), 5–40.

Caputo, J. (1987). *Radical hermeneutics: Repetition, deconstruction, and the hermeneutic project.* Bloomington: University of Indiana Press.

Center for Media Education. (1996). And now a WEB from our sponsor: How online advertisers are cashing in on our children. (http://epn.org/cme/infoactive/22/22nweb.html).

Christ, W. G., & Potter, W. J. (1998). Media literacy, media education, and the academy. *Journal of Communication*, 48(1), 5–15.

Cobb, C. (1997, April 20). Snaring kids in the Net: Firms use Web to sell alcohol, smokes to youth. *The Gazette* (Montreal), A1.

Collins, A. (1994). Intellectuals, power, and quality television. In H. Giroux & P. McLaren (Eds.), *Between borders: Pedagogy and the politics of cultural studies* (pp. 56–73). New York: Routeledge.

Collins, S. (1997, downloaded July 16). Web66: A fear of rare and mysterious dangers. (http://web66.coled.umn.edu/Ramble/ChildSafety.html).

Committee on Commerce & Committee on Education and the Workforce (1998, September). *Education and technology initiatives* (ISBN 0-16-057671-7). Washington, DC: U.S. Government Printing Office.

Considine, D. M. (1990, December). Media literacy: Can we get there from here? *Educational Technology*, 19, 7–19.

Considine, D., & Haley, G. (1992). *Visual messages: Integrating imagery into instruction*. Englewood, CO: Teacher Ideas Press.

Crossman, D. (1997). The evolution of the World Wide Web as an emerging instructional technology tool. In B. H. Khan (Ed.), *Web-based instruction*. Englewood Cliffs, NJ: Educational Technology Publications.

DeFalco, J. (1996, August 18). Cyber seducers? Advertising on the Internet. *Information Access Company*, 28(4), 54.

DeGaetano, G., & Bander, K. (1996). *Screen smarts: A family guide to media literacy*. Boston: Houghton Mifflin.

Dejevsky, M. (1998, June 5). Laws sought for children's privacy on Internet. *The Independent* (London), 9.

Dewey, J. (1985). *The public and its problems*. Chicago: Swallow Press.

Dorr, A., & Brannon, C. (1992, March 18–20). Media education in American schools at the end of the twentieth century. In *Media competency as a challenge to school and education: A German–North American dialogue: Compendium of a conference held by the Bertelsmann Foundation*. Gutersloh, Germany.

Douglas, S. (1994). *Where the girls are: Growing up female with the mass media*. New York: Random House.

Ellsworth, E. (1989). Why doesn't this feel empowering? In C. Luke & J. Gore (Eds.), *Feminisms and critical pedagogy* (pp. 90–119). New York: Routledge.

Ertel, M., & Valauskas, E. J. (Eds.). (1996). *The Internet for teachers and school library media specialists: Today's applications, tomorrow's prospects*. New York: Neal-Schuman.

Evans-Pritchard, A. (1997, March 16). White House saw radar tapes before NTSB. *International News Electronic Telegraph* (pp. 4–5). (www.access one.com/-rivero/crash/twa/news.html#ww_11_18).

Falanga, R. E. (1996). Childhood's end: Visions of the Internet. In M. Ertel & E. J. Valauskas (Eds.), *The Internet for teachers and school library media specialists: Today's applications, tomorrow's prospects* (pp. 3–14). New York: Neal-Schuman.

Fisher, B. A. (1987). *Interpersonal communication: Pragmatics of human relationships*. New York: Random House.

Fitzsimmons-Hunter, P., & Moran, C. (1998). Writing teachers, schools, access, and change. In T. Taylor & I. Ward (Eds.), *Literacy theory in the age of the Internet* (pp. 158–169). New York: Columbia University Press.

Flaherty, J. (1998, October 7). Racist e-mail is sent to 13 at Boston College. *New York Times*, B8.

Frechette, J. (1997). The politics of implementing media literacy into the United States: A look at the objectives and obstacles facing the Massachusetts public school teacher. Master's thesis, Department of Communication, University of Massachusetts, Amherst.

Freire, P. (1985). *The politics of education: Culture, power, and liberation*. South Hadley, MA: Bergin & Garvey.

———. (1989). *Pedagogy of the oppressed*. New York: Continuum.

Garner, R., & Gillingham, M. G. (1996). *Internet communications in six classrooms: Conversations across time, space, and culture*. Mahwah, NJ: Lawrence Erlbaum.

Gee, J. (1991). What is literacy? In C. Mitchell and K. Weiler (Eds.), *Rewriting literacy: Culture and the discourse of the other*. New York: Bergin & Garvey.

Gerbner, G., Gross, L., Jackson-Beeck, M., Jeffries-Fox, S., & Signorielli, N. (1978). Cultural indicators: Violence profile no. 9. *Journal of Communication*, 30, 10–29.

Giroux, H. (1992). *Border crossings: Cultural workers and the politics of education*. New York: Routledge.

———. (1996). Is there a place for cultural studies in colleges of education? In H. Giroux, C. Lankshear, P. McLaren, & M. Peters (Eds.), *Counternarratives: Cultural studies and critical pedagogies in postmodern spaces* (pp. 41–58). New York: Routledge.

Giroux, H., & McLaren, P. (1989). *Critical pedagogy, the state, and cultural struggle*. Albany: SUNY.

———. (1994), *Between borders: Pedagogy and the politics of cultural studies*. New York: Routledge.

Giroux, H., & Simon, R. (Eds.). (1989). *Popular culture, schooling, and everyday life*. Granby, MA: Bergin & Garvey.

Gordon, D. R. (1971). *The new literacy*. Toronto: University of Toronto Press.

Gramsci, A. (1971). *Selections from the Prison Notebooks*. New York: International Publishers.

Grossberg, L. (1994). Introduction: Bringin' it all back home—Pedagogy and cultural studies. In H. Giroux & P. McLaren (Eds.), *Between borders: Pedagogy and the politics of cultural studies* (pp. 1–25). New York: Routledge.

Grossberg, L., Nelson, C., & Triechler, P. (Eds.). (1992). *Cultural studies*. New York: Routledge.

Habermas, J. (1989). *The structural transformation of the public sphere*. Cambridge, MA: MIT Press.

Hall, S. (1980). Encoding/decoding. In S. Hall, D. Hobson, A. Lowe, & P. Willis (Eds.), *Culture, media, language* (pp. 128–138). London: Hutchinson.

———. (1981). Notes on deconstructing "the popular." In R. Samuel (Ed.), *People's history and socialist theory*. London: Routledge and Kegan Paul.

———. (1986). Popular culture and the state. In T. Bennett, C. Mercer, & J. Woollacott (Eds.), *Popular culture and social relations* (pp. 22–49). Milton Keynes: Open University Press.

———. (1992). Cultural studies and its theoretical legacies. In L. Grossberg, C. Nelson, & P. Treichler (Eds.), *Cultural studies* (pp. 277–285). New York: Routledge.

———. (1993). What is this "black" in black popular culture? In Deck, G. (Ed.), *Black popular culture* (pp. 21–36). Seattle: Bay Press.

Hirsch, E. D. (1987). *Cultural literacy*. Boston: Houghton Mifflin.

Hobbs, R. (1997). Literacy for the information age. In J. Flood, S. B. Heath, & D. Lapp (Eds.), *Handbook of research on teaching literacy through the communicative and visual arts* (pp. 7–14). New York: Simon & Schuster Macmillan.

———. (1998). Critically analyzing Internet Web sites. *The Re-Visioning Project final report: Teaching humanities in a media age*. Worcester, MA: Clark University, Summer Institute for Secondary School Educators.

———. (1998, Winter). The seven great debates in the media literacy movement. *Journal of Communication*, 16–32.

Houk, A., & Bogart, C. (1974). *Media literacy: Thinking about*. Dayton, OH: Plaum/Standard.

Itzkoff, S. W. (1969). *Cultural pluralism and American education*. Scranton, PA: International Press.

Jasper, W. (1997). What happened to TWA 800? (pp. 9–17). (www.accessone. com/-rivero/crash/twa/news.html#ww_11_18).

Kanpol, B. (1997). *Issues and trends in critical pedagogy*. Cresskill, NJ: Hampton Press.

Kelly, M. R. (1983). *A parents' guide to television: Making the most of it*. New York: Wiley.

Kozol, J. (1991). *Savage inequalities: Children in America's schools*. New York: Crown.

Kubey, R. (1998, Winter). Obstacles to the development of media education in the United States. *Journal of Communication*, 58–69.

Laclau, E., & Mouffe, C. (1985). *Hegemony and socialist strategy: Towards a radical democratic politics*. London: Verso.

Landow, G. P. (1992). *Hypertext: The convergence of contemporary critical theory and technology*. Baltimore: Johns Hopkins University Press.

Lanham, R. A. (1993). *The electronic word: Democracy, teaching, and the arts*. Chicago: University of Chicago Press.

Lankshear, C., Peters, M., & Knobel, M. (1996). Critical pedagogy and cyberspace. In H. Giroux, C. Lankshear, P. McLaren, and M. Peters (Eds.), *Counternarratives: Cultural studies and critical pedagogies in postmodern spaces* (pp. 149–188). New York: Routledge.

Lansham, R. A. (1992). Digital rhetoric: Theory, practice, and property. In M. Tuman (Ed.), *Literacy online: The promise (and peril) of reading and writing with computers* (pp. 221–244). Pittsburgh: University of Pittsburgh Press.

Lather, P. (1991). *Getting smart: Feminist research and pedagogy with/in the postmodern*. New York: Routledge.

Leavis, F. R., & Thompson, D. (1933). *Culture and environment: The training of critical awareness.* London: Chatto & Windus.

Leveranz, D, & Tyner, K. (1993, August/September). Inquiring minds want to know: What is media literacy? *The Independent,* 21–25.

Lewis, J., & Jhally, S. (1998, Winter). The struggle over media literacy. *Journal of Communication,* 109–120.

Lewis, P. (1996, March 1). Microsoft backs ratings system for Internet. (www.bilkent.edu.tr/pub/www/pics/960228/nytimes.html).

Maddison, J. (1971). *Radio and television in literacy: A survey of the use of the broadcasting media in combating literacy among adults.* Paris: UNESCO.

Manley-Casimer, M. E., & Luke, C. (Eds.). (1987). *Children and television: A challenge for education.* New York: Praeger.

Massachusetts Department of Education. (1994, September). State Publication No. 17608-14-100,000.

Masterman, L. (1985). *Teaching the media.* London: Comedia.

McLaren, P. (1988). Foreword: Critical theory and the meaning of hope. In H. Giroux (Ed.), *Teachers as intellectuals* (pp. ix–xxi). Granby, MA: Bergin & Garvey.

———. (1989). *Life in schools.* New York: Longman.

McLuhan, M. (1964). *Understanding media: The extensions of man.* New York: McGraw-Hill.

*Media Literacy Resource Guide.* (1989). Ontario: Ministry of Education.

Mendels, P. (1998, October 15). Schools train students to staff computer help desks. (www.yte.org/article4.htm).

Messaris, P. (1994). *Visual "literacy": Image, mind, and reality.* Boulder, CO: Westview Press.

———. (1998, Winter). Visual aspects of media literacy. *Journal of Communication,* 70–80.

Meyrowitz, J. (1998, Winter). Multiple media literacies. *Journal of Communication,* 96–108.

Mifflin, L. (1997, April 21). New guidelines on Net ads for children. *New York Times,* D5.

Mohanty, C. T. (1994). On race and voice: Challenges for liberal education in the 1990s. In H. Giroux & P. McLaren (Eds.), *Between borders: Pedagogy and the politics of cultural studies* (pp. 145–166). New York: Routledge.

Morgan, M., & Signorielli, N. (1990). Cultivation analysis: Conceptualization and methodology. In M. Morgan and N. Signorielli (Eds.), *Cultivation analysis: New directions in media effects research* (pp. 13–34). Newbury Park, CA: Sage.

Mouffe, C. (1993). *The return of the political.* London: Verso.

New London Group. (1996). A pedagogy of multiliteracies: Designing social futures. *Harvard Educational Review,* 66(1), 60–92.

Osborne, R., & Freyberg, P. (1985). *Learning in science: The implications of children's science.* Portsmouth, NH: Heinemann.

Paul, R. (1995). Critical thinking: How to prepare students for a rapidly changing world. In R. Paul and J. Willsen (Eds.), *Accelerating change, the com-*

*plexity of problems, and the quality of our thinking.* Rohnert Park, CA: Foundation for Critical Thinking.

Phillips, P., & Project Censored (2001). *Censored 2001.* New York: Seven Stories Press.

Ploghoft, M. E., & Anderson, J. A. (Eds.). (1981). *Education for the television age.* Springfield, IL: Charles C. Thomas.

Postman, N. (1993). *Technopoly: The surrender of culture to technology.* New York: Alfred Knopf.

―――. (1995). *The end of education: Redefining the value of school.* New York: Vintage Books.

Potter, J., and Wetherell, M. (1987). *Discourse and social psychology: Beyond attitudes and behaviour.* London: Sage.

Quesada, A., & Lockwood Summers, S. (1998, January). Literacy in the cyberage: Teaching kids to be media savvy. *Technology & Learning,* 18(5), 30–36.

Rajasingham, L., & Tiffin, J. (1995). *In search of the virtual class: Education in an information society.* London: Routledge.

Resnick, P. (1997, March). Filtering information on the Internet. *Scientific American,* 106–108.

Rheingold, H. (1994). *The virtual community: Finding connection in a computerized world.* London: Secker & Warburg.

Robins, K. (1996). Cyberspace and the world we live in. In J. Dovey (Ed.), *Fractal dreams: New media in social context* (pp. 1–30). London: Lawrence & Wishart.

Roerden, L. P. (1997). *Net lessons: Web-based projects for your classroom.* Sebastol, CA: Songline Studios.

Safdar, S. J., & Cherry, S. (1995–1996). Internet Parental Control Frequently Asked Questions provided by the Voters Telecommunications Watch. (www.vtw.org/parents).

Scheunemann, D. (Ed.). (1996). *Orality, literacy, and modern media.* Columbia, SC: Camden House.

Schiesel, S. (1997, March 7). The media business: On Web, new threats seen to the young. *New York Times,* A1.

Schramm, W. (1977). *Big media, little media: Tools and Technologies for Instruction.* Beverly Hills and London: Sage.

Schwoch, J., White, M., & Reilly, S. (1992). *Media knowledge: Readings in popular culture, pedagogy, and critical citizenship.* Albany: State University of New York Press.

Scott, T., Cole, M., & Engel, M. (1992). Computers and education: A cultural constructivist perspective. In G. Grant (Ed.), *Review of research in education* (vol. 18, pp. 191–251). Washington, DC: American Educational Research Association.

Scribner, S., & Cole, M. (1981). *The psychology of literacy.* Cambridge: Harvard University Press.

Shaefer, D. (1995). Media literacy in the communication age: Some thoughts on the dialogic aspects of multimedia technologies. Paper presented for course Comm: 850 at Ohio State University.

Sholle, D., & Denski, S. (1994). *Media education and the (re)production of culture*. Westport, CT: Bergin & Garvey.

Shor, I. (1992). *Empowering education: Critical teaching for social change*. Chicago: University of Chicago Press.

Sinatra, R. (1986). *Visual literacy connections to thinking, reading, and writing*. Springfield, IL: Charles C. Thomas.

Sistek-Chandler, C. (1999, February). To HTML or not to HTML? *Converge*, pp. 14–18.

Spivak, G., with Rooney, E. (1989). In a word. Interview. *differences* 1 (20): 124–156.

Stoll, C. (1995). *Silicon snake oil: Second thoughts on the information highway*. New York: Anchor Books.

Strommen, E. (1995, November 1). Television catches its second wave: Classroom TV and video evolve from passive instruments to interactive tools. *Electronic Learning*, 15(3), 30.

Talbott, S. L. (1995). *The future does not compute: Transcending the machines in our midst*. Sebastopol, CA: O'Reilly & Associates.

Taylor, T., & Ward, I. (Eds.). (1998). *Literacy theory in the age of the Internet*. New York: Columbia University Press.

Thoman, E. (1998). *Skills and strategies for media education*. (Available from the Center for Media Literacy, 4727 Wilshire Blvd., Ste. 403, Los Angeles, CA 90010).

Trotter, A. (2001, January). New law directs schools to install Internet filtering devices. *Education Week*, 20(16), 32.

Tuman, M. C. (1992). First thoughts. In M. Tuman (Ed.), *Literacy online: The promise (and peril) of reading and writing with computers* (pp. 3–15). Pittsburgh: University of Pittsburgh Press.

Tyner, K. (1998). *Literacy in a digital world: Teaching and learning in the age of information*. Mahwah, NJ: Lawrence Erlbaum.

Warschauer, M. (1999). *Electronic literacies: Language, culture, and power in online education*. Mahwah, NJ: Lawrence Erlbaum.

Williamson, J. (1992). How does girl number twenty understand ideology? In M. Alvarado & O. Boyd-Barrett (Eds.), *Media education: An introduction* (pp. 83–84). London: British Film Institute.

Willis, P. (1977). *Learning to labor: How working-class kids get working-class jobs*. New York: Columbia University Press.

Zettl, H. (1998, Winter). Contextual media aesthetics as the basis for media literacy. *Journal of Communication*, 81–95.

# Index

Adorno, Theodor, 38
advertising: children and, 13; Children's Advertising Review Unit (CARU), 14–15, 52; on cyber safesites, 50–56; online advertising, 13–18
Althusser, Louis, 37
America Online (AOL), 46
"And Now a WEB from Our Sponsor: How Online Advertisers Are Cashing In on Children" (CME), 13
Aronowitz, Stanley, 5
art/graphic design and music, 63, 109, 128
artificial intelligence, 3
assessment practices, 65, 130–131
audioconferencing, 7
audiovisual technology, 2

Becker, Henry, 5
*Between Borders* (Grossberg), 34
Birmingham School of British Cultural Studies, 37
Bloom, Benjamin S., 57, 118
Bloom's taxonomy, 66, 71, 83, 118–119, 133

Bolter, Jay David, 69
Bracey, Bonnie, 10
Brannon, Craig, 75–76
Bransford, John D., 57, 66, 118
Bruce, Bertram, 9
Buckingham, David, 32, 76
Burbules, Nicholas, 18–19
business communities, 63–63, 127–128

Campeau, Peggy, 1–2
Caputo, John, 114
Center for Media Education (CME), 13, 17–18
Channel One, 11, 50
chat room for children, 14
Children's Advertising Review Unit (CARU), 14–15, 52
Chris, William, 31–32, 120
civic arena, 113
Cole, Michael, 5
Collins, Stephen, 18–19
Communications Decency Act, 48, 55
Competitive Enterprise Institute, 16
computer technology, 36; curriculum

and, 6–7; education and, 1–7; pedagogical strategy for, 83; as tool, 5
Concord Consortium, 69
Considine, David, 86
content literacy, 76–77, 79, 84–85
content skills, 77
critical autonomy, 29–30, 36, 56. *See
  also* empowerment
critical cultural studies, 36–40
critical pedagogy, 32–36, 39; in cyberspace, 7–11; defined, 32–33;
  goals of, 32–34; information, and, 8–
  9; knowledge and, 8–9; student-
  teachers and, 111–112;
  understanding and, 8–9
"Critical Theory and the Meaning of
  Hope" (McLaren), 32
critical thinking, research methods of
  achieving, 66
*Critical Thinking* (Paul), 82
Crossman, David, 84
cultivation analysis, 28
*Cultural Literacy* (Hirsch), 2
cultural studies, 37–38
Culture and Environment (Leavis
  and Thompson), 32
curriculum: computer technology
  and, 6–7; designing cyber-literacy
  lessons, 88–92; integrating computers into, 76, 106–110, 119–120;
  "multi-literacy" curricular models,
  79; technology-based literacy
  program, 73–74. *See also* Lighthouse Technology Grants
cyber-interactions, 93
cyber-literacy lessons: across subjects, 76, 106–110; analysis of media, 89–90; design of, 88–92;
  integration into curriculum, 76,
  106–110, 119–120; Lesson 1, 92–
  98; Lesson 2, 98–100; Lesson 3,
  100–101; Lesson 4, 101–106;
  research sources, 90–91
cyber-media: critical pedagogy in, 7–
  11; future of, 120–122; online advertisers, 13; political economy of,
  13–21
CyberPatrol, 44, 49, 53–54, 56, 118

Cybersitter, 44, 49
cybersurfing skills, 93

DeFalco, Julie, 14, 16–19
Denski, Stan, 30, 33, 36, 74n, 114
Dewey, John, 110, 113
dialogical model of pedagogy, 34
Dorr, Aimee, 75–76
Douglas, Susan, 97

e-mail, 9
educational funding, 6
Educational Technology (EdTech) initiatives, 68, 119, 121
Educational Testing Service, 6
Ellsworth, Elizabeth, 111–113
*Empowering Education* (Shor), 36
empowerment, 32, 34, 72–73; Shor's
  student-centered learning, 110–
  111
Engel, Martin, 5

Federal Trade Commission (FTC), 13
foreign language/ESL, 64, 129
Freire, Paulo, 33, 72
Freyberg, Peter, 57, 66, 118

Garner, Ruth, 4–6, 9–10, 11n
geography, 108
Gerbner, George, 37
Gillingham, Mark, 4–6, 9–10, 11n
Giroux, Henry, 8, 33, 35, 39, 72
global village, 4
grammar literacy, 77
Gramsci, Antonio, 37, 39, 51
Grossberg, Lawrence, 34, 115
Grossberg's pedagogy of risk and ar-
  ticulation, 35

Habermas, Jurgen, 20
Haley, Gail, 86
Hall, Stuart, 37–38
health, 109
hierarchical model, 34
Hirsch, E. D., 2–3
Hobbs, Renée, 32, 116n
Horkheimer, Max, 38
"How Does Girl Number Twenty Un-

derstand Ideology" (Williamson), 98

*In Search of the Virtual Class* (Rajasingham and Tiffin), 7
Independent Media Center (IMC), 101
instructional media; effectiveness of learning and, 1–2; television, 7
interdisciplinary projects, 64, 129–130
Internet: chat rooms for children, 14; child safety and, 18–19; classroom teacher and, 9; corporate sites, 14–15; funding inequalities, 5; as global community, 4; inappropriate content, 43; marketing on "cyber safe-sites," 50–56; online advertising, 13–18; parental guidance and, 44–45; personal information on, 14, 18; proof-of-age/shielding systems, 45; restrictions and resources, 43–56; safety issues, 43; unequal access to, 5
*Internet Communications in Six Classrooms* (Garner and Gillingham), 9
Internet content: content filtering, 45; freedom of expression and, 45, 108; inappropriate content in schools, 46–50; responses to, 44–46; student code of conduct, 46–47
Internet Filter, 48
Internet Parental Control (IPC), 44–45, 50
Internet Voluntary Self-Rating (IVSR), 48
*Issues and Trends in Critical Pedagogy* (Kanpol), 33

Jasper, William, 104

Kanpol, Barry, 33–34
Knobel, Michele, 8–10, 13, 20, 69
Kozol, Jonathan, 6
Kubey, Robert, 82

Laclau, E., 39
Landow, George, 69
language arts, 59, 63–68, 106, 123–124
Lanham, Richard, 69
Lankshear, Colin, 8–10, 13, 20, 69
Lascoutx, Elizabeth, 15
Lather, Patti, 114
Leavis, F. R., 32
Leveranz, Deborah, 30
Lewis, Peter, 54
Lighthouse Technology Grants, 57–65, 118, 121; art/graphic design and music, 63, 128; assessment practices, 65, 130–131; business communities and, 63, 127–128; foreign language/ESL, 64, 129; hardware components, 60; implications of, 65–68; interdisciplinary projects, 64, 129–130; language arts, 59, 63–68, 123–124; mathematics projects, 61–62, 127; project summaries, 123–131; purpose and nature of, 57–58; research findings, 58–65; science projects, 61, 125–126; social studies projects, 62, 126–127; special education programs, 65, 128–129; summary of projects, 59; technology projects, 60, 124–125
literacy: conceptualizing a technology-based program, 73–74; cultural knowledge base, 2–3; technological change vs., 3
*Literacy in a Digital World* (Tyner), 1
*Literacy Online* (Tuman), 2
Lockwood Summers, Sue, 82, 88–89, 92

McLaren, Peter, 32–33, 35, 72
McLuhan, Marshall, 4, 29, 78
marketing, on cyber safe-sites, 50–56
mass media, defined, 25
Massachusetts Department of Education (DOE), 68, 70–71, 119
Masterman, Len, 29–30, 36, 56
mathematics projects, 61–62, 107, 127

media: adult education and, 1; corporate ownership of, 27; defined, 25; social/political implications of, 28. *See also* media literacy
media artists, 30–31
media content, 82
media content literacy, 83–86
media education: critical autonomy and, 29–30; objectives of, 30; primary goal of, 29
*Media Education and the (Re)Production of Culture* (Sholle and Denski), 33
media grammar literacy, 82, 86–87
media literacy, 20; awareness of social/political effects, 28; basic questions/concepts of, 99; building blocks of, 23–29; in classroom, 81; commercial implications of, 27; compare/contrast of forms, 80; conceptual issues/debates of, 31–32; content literacy, 76–77, 79; criticism of, 24; cyber-ventures futures, 120–122; defined, 24–25; goals and approaches of, 29–36; grammar literacy, 77; ideological/value messages, 27–28; key concepts, 26; media construct reality, 26; medium literacy, 78, 87–88; multiple media literacies, 76–82
*Media Literacy in the Communication Age* (Shaefer), 20
medium literacy, 78, 87–88
medium theory, 82
Mendels, Pamela, 71
Meyrowitz, Joshua, 76–79, 81, 84–85, 87, 119
Mifflin, Lawrie, 14
Model Nets, 2
Montgomery, Kathryn C., 15
Mouffe, Chantal, 35, 39
multi-literacies, 79
multiculturalism, 34
multiple media literacies, 76–82

National Center for Education Statistics, 5

National Information Infrastructure Advisory Council, 10
Net Nanny, 44, 48, 52, 56, 118
New London Group, 77

online advertising, 13–18
Osborne, Roger, 57, 66, 118

Pasnik, Shelly, 17
Paul, Richard, 82
personal empowerment. *See* empowerment
Peters, Michael, 8–10, 13, 20, 69
Platform for Internet Content Selection (PICS), 44, 47–48, 53, 56
political economy, 27; cybermedia and, 13–21
popular culture, 36–40, 98
Postman, Neil, 4
Potter, W. James, 31–32, 120
praxical pedagogy, 34
production values (encoding), 93
progressive pedagogy, hierarchical model, 34

Quesada, Arli, 82, 88–89, 92

Rajasingham, Lalita, 3–4, 7–8, 69
Recreational Software Advisory Council on the Internet (RSACi), 44, 47–48, 53–55, 118
Rehingold, Howard, 121
Resnick, Paul, 48, 55–56
Roerden, Laura Parker, 10

SafeSurf, 51–52, 56, 118
Salinger, Pierre, 102
Schiesel, Seth, 15–16
Schramm, Wilbur, 2
science projects, 61, 107, 125–126
Scott, Tony, 5
Shaefer, David, 20
Sholle, David, 30, 33, 36, 74n, 114
Shor, Ira, 34–36, 72–73, 110, 115
Simon, Roger, 33, 39
social studies projects, 62, 107–108, 126–127

special education programs, 65, 128–
  129
Spivak, Gayatri, 114
sports and recreation, 109
staff development, 76
Stewart, Alex, 48
Strommen, Erik, 16
student-centered learning, 10, 110
student code of conduct for Internet,
  46–47
Surfwatch, 44, 49, 53–54

Taylor, Todd, 10
teacheras facilitator, 10; Internet
  and, 9
*Teaching the Media* (Masterman), 29
technological change, literacy vs., 3
Technology Literacy Challenge Fund,
  57
technology projects, 60, 124–125
*Technopoly* (Postman), 4
telecommunications, 13
telecourses, 69
telelearning, 7–8
telestudent, 4, 69
Thoman, Elizabeth, 56
Thompson, Denys, 32
Tiffin, John, 3–4, 7–8, 69
Tuman, Myron, 2–3
Tyner, Kathleen, 1–2, 6, 30, 115, 121

U.S. Department of Education, 68

Varney, Christine A., 15
VHS: Virtual High School project, 68–
  70, 119; criticism of, 69–70; positive feedback of, 69
video equipment, 36
video production, 115
virtual class, 4, 7, 110–116
virtual playrooms, 13–21
*Visual Messages* (Considine and Haley), 86
Vye, Nancy J., 57, 66, 118

Ward, Irene, 10
Warschauer, Mark, 3, 5, 10, 11n
Web-based lesson plans, 10; *See also*
  curriculum
Web sites, construction/analysis of,
  93–97
*Where the Girls Are* (Douglas), 97
Williamson, Judith, 94, 98
Willis, Paul, 38
World Trade Organization (WTO),
  101

YTE: Youth Tech Entrepreneurs, 70–
  73, 119; market-driven technology
  program and, 72; student as labor,
  71

**ABOUT THE AUTHOR**

JULIE D. FRECHETTE is an Assistant Professor in the Department of Communications at Worcester State College. She is the coauthor of the "Media Literacy and Gender Equity Curriculum" (1999), distributed to teachers in the state of Massachusetts.